Sue Nickel writes from deep within the crucible of depression. Yet she is remarkably able to come up with a strong, positive, faith-based story of supportive encouragement and hope. She acknowledges the many difficulties of recognizing oneself in these depths, but she also brings out the many facets of recovery that are possible.

—Dr. Lorne Brandt, Psychiatrist, MD, FRCP

Be Held is a daily companion full of lived understanding, hope, and grace that can accompany and support you, or someone you love or care for, through a depressive period. Sue Nickel's personal walk with mental illness is told in a way to bring comfort through knowledge, insight, and faith to others. This is a book to hold onto and share.

—Terresa Augustine, MA
Programming Director, Sanctuary Mental Health Society
Mental Health First Aid Instructor

Ideal for an 8 week medication trial

Be Held

Daily Inspiration When Facing Depression

SUE NICKEL

Printed in Canada

ISBN: 978-1-4866-1641-1

Word Alive Press
119 De Baets Street Winnipeg, MB R2J 3R9
www.wordalivepress.ca

Cataloguing in Publication information can be obtained from Library and Archives Canada.

To my husband,
Dieter

And to our children,
Haida, Jesse, Liana, Keith, and Jenna

All glory to God,
Creator,
Redeemer,
and
Lifter of my head

Acknowledgements

WHEN WRITING ABOUT ONE'S LIFE, HOW ARE ALL THOSE WHO have graced it appropriately noted and thanked? This is a blessed dilemma, so I shall start from the beginning.

My parents, Betty Ann and Jim Knickerbocker, had high expectations of us children, but their levels of love and support were incredibly high as well. They cheered, mentored, laughed, listened, lent shoulders to cry upon, and buoyed us throughout the years. Heartfelt thanks to you, Mom and Dad, for your undying, gracious, and unshakable love. I thank my brother, Paul, for his unconditional companionship while we were growing up—you were my world. And heartfelt thanks go to my sister, Nancy, for her fierce and steadfast sistership. She (adamantly) helped me believe in myself these past twenty years as I grew up and finally believed that I, too, could be beautiful.

Special thanks also go to my adopted family, Rita and Arthur Block and their lovely, lively clan. Their home was full of respectful care and predictability; it was my safe landing place. All my love to you always, Les. Thank you for sharing.

I thank my mother and father in-law with humble gratitude for welcoming me into the family. I thank them for their laughter and their love for one another. Their marriage was an inspiration to us all and a constant encouragement, a frame for me of steadfastness and loyalty.

I also extend my deep, heartfelt gratitude to my pastors, Palmer Becker, for his love of ordered, spontaneous worship, and Ardys, for her lovely humility; Laura and Sven Eriksson, for their loving patience and teaching me about grace through their constant embodiment of it; and Sandra and Tim Kuepfer, for living out Christ's peace and social justice time and time again, calling me forward, calling me onward. I also thank my new friends, Pastor Winston Pratt and Sharon, with whom wonderful moments of friendship and worship have already taken place. I have been greatly blessed by my church family, which has consistently supported and nurtured me along this road of lived experience and recovery. Hours have been spent listening, many moments have been spent praying, and even when I haven't been there for weeks I have felt mysteriously connected. Thank you.

My stories have been healed as they have been heard. I owe a great deal of thanks to Sue Diamond Potts, RCC, for her compassion and wisdom as I redefined much of my life in her nonjudgmental, encouraging presence. I met Colin Cash, MSW, on the psychiatric ward in 2003 and am grateful for how I have been so generously supported, respected, and celebrated since then. I have learned much. I am humbled by his graciousness and thankful for this safe man in my life.

There are several key friendships in our lives and in our families that have meant the world to Dieter and me. Your words of encouragement, cards, care, prayers, and concern have been the scaffold upholding and containing us throughout some very difficult years. I trust you know who you are, and I pray you will know how we love you so.

To my readers: Terresa Augustine, Dr. Lorne Brandt, and Rosalie Niebuhr. Thank you for your time, honesty, hard work, and loveliness. Most of all, thank you for the gift of having three people in my life with whom I can trust to be so vulnerable.

To two very fine women at Word Alive Press: Sylvia St. Cyr and Marina Reis. Many thanks to you both for your hard work, with special thanks for answering my many questions so graciously, even when the answer was right in front of my eyes. Your lovely posture and responses to my limitations were so welcome and relieving, they made my heart smile.

Evan Braun at Word Alive Press has been my very first editor, and if the future editors of my life are half as gracious

I will be a blessed woman indeed. Thank you, Evan; I have learned a great deal, and having you as the one to refine and redefine *Be Held* has been a sincere privilege. To the several other fine members of Word Alive Press who have contributed creativity, beauty, and integrity to the shaping of *Be Held*, I am humbled and deeply grateful.

In my present work I am held and cheered on by the wonderful team at Sanctuary Mental Health Society in Vancouver. We share the awesome vocation of mental health advocacy and all the people at Sanctuary—with special mention of Terresa, Kate, Dan, and Sharon—have made this work a holy privilege. Blessed am I to call you dear friends.

I truly do not have adequate words to express my intense gratitude for the twenty-plus years of care I have received from my neuropsychiatrist, Dr. Trevor Hurwitz. It is a very unique relationship, this staggering dependence upon and absolute trust in one individual that at times has literally been my lifeline. I don't much like needing someone to this degree, but he has always been a safe and honorable man of integrity who fights for me. I am eternally indebted.

My sweet, dear children and children-in-law have brought many moments of light into my life. I struggle with depression in the best possible circumstances because of this generation and the next. Thank you, Haida, Jesse, Liana, Keith, and Jenna—you give me reasons to live. And to your little people? Ah, ten thousand-fold blessings! How is such love possible? My heart chokes on it with fierce protection. They are *love* and *light* immeasurable.

Most of all, it has been my husband who has been integral to my recovery. Never allowing me to play the victim, he has maintained a level of expectancy wherein I was unable to just check out and go underground into my darkness. I haven't always liked or appreciated this, but Dieter continually placed before me a picture of me as a functioning and contributing adult. He frequently showed me that I had capabilities, and that, for the most part, I could trust myself. Thank you, dearest one, for showing me life when I could see none, and for helping me choose it. Thank you for upholding "in sickness and in health." Thank you for choosing to constantly redefine life.

Introduction

THIS BOOK IS, PRIMARILY, AN EIGHT-WEEK JOURNEY TO COME alongside you as you try out a new antidepressant or other psychiatric medication. Written from a Christian perspective, it is meant to support and encourage you as you wait out the weeks to see if your medication is going to be effective.

If you are taking an antidepressant for the very first time, how brave of you! If this is your fourth or fifth medication trial, hang in there; I've been there and know the discouragement and dismay.

But the book is by no means intended solely for eight weeks and new medications. My hope is that readers who are experiencing depression will find my writings inspiring, comforting, and encouraging for any days at all.

This book contains fifty-six readings to get you through the trial of discovering if your specific medication is going to help. I pray that it does. You can read through my book day after day if you like; sometimes the predictability of a ritual is soothing. For others, it may be too stressful to have to read a section every day. Try things out and find out what works best for you, no one else. Don't compare, and don't worry about how others do it. Just do the readings in the way they work for you. I would suggest that if you feel pretty scattered in your head, it would be beneficial to stick with the readings in the first third of the book for a while; they're less reflective, more concrete, and shorter.

At some point you may wish to read something on a particular topic, such as grace or hope. Each day's writing speaks to one or more of this book's key themes—comfort, grace, hope, information, joy, and suffering—which are labelled just under the titles. A full list of which entries fall into which themes can be found at the back of the book.

You'll also notice that the readings are not the same in length. This is purposeful, as some days you are able to concentrate for longer periods of time than others. Therefore, for those days when you are feeling particularly restless or fatigued, and desire a shorter reading, you can find a list of short items at the end of the book as well.

As a final note, although there is some psychiatric and psychological learning to be gained through the readings, this is not an academic book. There are many books that explain the biology of depression, so my desire has been to write a book that reflects my experience of *living with* the biology, explains how it affected me socially and psychologically, and explores what it meant for my relationship with our Trinitarian God and my efforts to remain part of my faith community.

The hardest part of depression for me is the distorted thoughts I often have about myself and life, and my worth in the world. I hope to offer some support and grace to you, the reader, as you seek to live with a disease that at times can be terrifying, and is most always exhausting.

God bless you as you journey through these coming weeks.

If the Lord had not been my help,
my soul would soon have lived in the land of silence.
When I thought, "My foot is slipping,"
your steadfast love, O Lord, held me up.
—Psalm 94:17–18

COMMON SIGNS AND SYMPTOMS OF DEPRESSION

- fatigue
- insomnia or sleeping too much
- overeating or loss of appetite
- weight loss or gain
- unexplained aches and pains
- decreased sexual desire
- lethargy
- sadness
- anger
- mood swings
- helplessness
- hopelessness
- anxiety
- feelings of being overwhelmed
- guilt
- shame and self-blame
- irritability
- atypical/unusual aggression
- social withdrawal
- difficulty making decisions
- ruminations
- suicidal ideation
- difficulty concentrating
- migraines
- neglecting responsibilities
- diminished memory

Preface

THE YEAR WAS 1994, AND AFTER MONTHS ON A WAITING LIST I WAS finally in his office. From my perspective across the desk, the infamous doctor appeared foreboding, even though he was neither tall nor bulky in stature. My mind was drenched in fear, and I deemed him immense with power because my life's healing was completely in his hands. I remember thinking he was probably a kind man, but after a short while I could no longer listen to him as his words—depression, medication, hospitalization—slapped at me and stung. I was struck dumb and unable to smile, which was unusual for me.

My diagnosis with clinical depression turned my world upside-down and filled me with a roaring rage. My life's dreams had once again been aborted. This stranger's empathy and care-filled manner had cracked my carefully constructed veneer and left me feeling raw and completely unhinged.

As I stood to leave several long moments later, he slipped a prescription paper into my hand.

"Take care," he said gently, "and I'll see you in six weeks."

Six weeks? Was he kidding? My world had just been shattered and now I was to be left alone in it for six weeks?

My throat's screams of loneliness echoed in my ears. My heart literally ached as I blindly put one foot in front of the other and began to leave. I scolded myself that I must not take up anymore of the important doctor's time.

And so I straightened my shoulders, shored up my courage, buttoned my black blazer, and covered my telling eyes with black-as-ink sunglasses before heading out. Above all, I was determined that no one outside would know what had happened inside. I would look and behave just like everyone else...

Week One

Day One: Taking Heart

Comfort

THE SCREAMING PAIN OF CHRONIC MIGRAINES IS WHAT INITIALLY propelled me into the doctor's office. If you had asked me if I felt down and constantly on the verge of tears, I would have tsked and scoffed, "Who wouldn't be, with crucifying pain in your head every day of the month?"

I was also constantly irritable, and getting out of bed in the morning was as difficult as wearing concrete bricks for slippers. I wanted to sleep all the time, but no matter how much I did I was always exhausted. My mind felt as thick as mud and I couldn't concentrate or make decisions.

What bothered me most, however, was how guilty and full of shame I constantly felt. I wore these feelings like a mantle, a heavy yoke that bowed me over. It was hard to lift my head.

What I didn't know was that my migraines were primarily due to an underlying clinical depression which had to be treated, my doctor said, before there could be any hope of lessening my headaches.

Does any of this sound familiar to you? Is this your experience, too, many days of the month?

Take heart, you are not alone: thousands and thousands of people all over the world feel exactly the same way. Perhaps you're at the point where you're admitting to yourself that things aren't so great and you think you need some help. Way to go! It's scary to admit that something's wrong; it's risky, because it probably means change of some kind, and who wants to change?

Speaking out and getting the help you need is a brave thing to do. So is admitting that you don't feel well and that you may need to slow down for a while and get some rest.

At the end of my first appointment with the psychiatrist, I felt so alone, with nothing to hang onto. I was aghast when he had said he would see me again in six weeks. Six l—o—o—n-n-g weeks. I hadn't known what he was sending me into, just that it wouldn't be to the same life I'd had when I had first walked into his office.

I needed something tangible to hang onto, something that would anchor me for the period of time until my next appointment.

The anxiety of that moment has never left me, and I've always wondered how I could help others who find themselves in the same situation. The following daily readings are an offering to help you manage your depression and its effects on your life as you heal and move towards health and wholeness. I hope they encourage you, help you to hang in there, and remind you, again and again, that you will not always feel this badly.

Don't think that you absolutely need to do a reading each day; just relax and do your best. This book is here for your support, and you know how that will best be served. If you miss a day or two, just return to reading when you're ready.

You can do this! I'm with you—not as someone who has done it perfectly, but as someone who's been there in the trenches for some twenty-odd years and has learned a few tricks.

> Try to give yourself the gift of this time, allowing your body, soul, and mind the rest they need to recover. Take heart: depression is a disease that is most often treated successfully. You will not always feel this badly, I promise. It may be a long road, but you will feel better, and your spirit for life will return.

Day Two: Like Any Other Organ,
Your Brain May Sometimes Need Help

Comfort/Information

DEPRESSION IS A MAJOR MOOD DISORDER, A NEUROLOGICAL brain disease that is no one's fault. Simply put, areas of your brain that regulate mood and your emotional experiences are compromised and in need of help. This is no different than when the pancreas of a person with diabetes is compromised or the intestines of someone with celiac disease are malfunctioning.

Our society finds it difficult to accept this logic, as if for some reason our brain—the greatest and most complex computer in the entire world—is a different kind of organ that shouldn't need medication. For those who don't agree with psychiatric medication, I want to ask you, why is it acceptable to take insulin because a person's pancreas cannot regulate their blood efficiently, but it's not acceptable to take a medication that will ensure therapeutic levels of brain neurotransmitters? These attitudes make it very difficult for people to admit to themselves and others how terribly awful they have been feeling.

> Depression is
> a major mood
> disorder, a
> neurological brain
> disease that is no
> one's fault.

But keep your chin up, because depression is a valid neuropsychiatric disorder—and it is all in your head. Literally! It's your brain that's involved, and your brain has a disease.

I find it helpful to reduce my responsibilities and get as much physical and emotional rest as possible. I try (and try) to go easy on myself despite the self-condemning and self-loathing voices inside my head. I also try to give myself a break regardless of other people's responses to my limits, and—perhaps most difficult of all—I try to be patient and remember that it takes six to eight weeks to determine the effectiveness of my medications.

> As you wait during these weeks, remember that the most important job you have is to rest and take care of yourself as your brain heals. Give yourself and your family this gift of time, and listen deeply for whisperings that all will be well.

Day Three:
A Chapter of Medication-Taking

Information

IF YOU HAVEN'T ALREADY DONE SO, START BY SEEING YOUR DOCTOR and explaining how you feel. If it's helpful, use the common symptoms listed at the front of this book. If the doctor diagnoses you with depression,[1] and if you have been prescribed an antidepressant medication, I encourage you to take it as directed. Your brain is an organ, and just like any other organ in your body it can become compromised

[1] I'm referring here to clinical depression, a neurological illness that affects mood for weeks, months, or years at a time. I'm not referring to the normal and appropriate grief that follows a significant loss in life. Although serious, clinical depression is usually treated successfully, and many people have only one or two episodes in their lifetime.

and need help. This takes patience, because the therapeutic effect of these medications isn't fully realized until six to eight weeks after the desired therapeutic dosage is reached. The process may go something like this:

- Your doctor may start you at a low dosage to allow time for your body to adjust to the medication. This may take one to two weeks.
- Only then does the six- to eight-week countdown begin. It doesn't begin the very first time you take the drug at the lowest dose.
- In other words, the entire time it takes to discover whether or not a certain medication is helpful for you can be ten weeks.

It is very important that you remain on your medication and take it as prescribed. You may not feel any improvement for some weeks, but things can turn around quickly at the end, so try your best to hang in there!

> Remember, this is a chapter in your life—a chapter, not the rest of your life. Depression is a diagnosis, not a noun that forever names who you are. You are, and forever will be, a beloved child of God who has nothing to prove right now and everything to rest for.

God is asking you, for a while, to give up all your virtuous yearnings and your callings—yes, even those in the name of the Lord—and rest in the arms of He who said,

"Come to me, all you that are weary and are carrying heavy burdens, and I will give you rest" (Matthew 11:28).

Trust this rest. Just try and rest into this rest.

Day Four:
Medications and Psychological Therapy

Information

MANY PEOPLE FIND IT DIFFICULT TO ACCEPT BEING ON psychiatric medication. My doctor has reported that when he meets a patient who has seizures, he schedules about fifteen minutes. Typically, epilepsy is easier to talk about than depression, and although some major adjustments are necessary, it doesn't come with the same shame and guilt that accompanies a mental illness.

When meeting a patient experiencing a depressive episode, he schedules twice as much time. Despite the statistics proclaiming that thousands of people are taking antidepressants, they are not doing so happily.

Although millions of prescriptions are being written, many thousands are not being filled. This can be due to a number of reasons, such as denial, fear, or lack of sufficient money and associated feelings of shame. Hence, some people are reluctant to return to their doctors and their recovery is effectively altered.

> My depression,
> like yours, was not
> my fault.

My first appointment with my psychiatrist took place in 1994 and I didn't truly comply with the recommended treatment until 1997. I was so sick by then that I couldn't work, keep up the household, or participate well in life in or outside our home. I seriously considered hospitalization, I closed down my counselling practice for four months, and I delegated my responsibilities to others. I became a homebound recluse.

These many years later, my own experience indicates, to me, that getting on and staying on medication as soon as possible is the best advice for when I'm experiencing moderate to severe depression.

My depression, like yours, was not my fault. But it felt like it was and I was ashamed. I thought I was lazy and I felt guilty, selfish, and weak for not being able to pull myself up by the bootstraps. More than twenty years later, I still have to remind myself that I have an illness, not a proclivity for laziness, cowardice, or a flawed personality.

Two therapies are excellent adjuncts to medication. First, *cognitive behavioral therapy* (CBT) helps us to work through the distorted thought processes that are commonly part of depression and often the root of our volatile feelings. Second, *interpersonal therapy* helps us to identify, understand, and resolve our conflicts with others. The benefit of connecting with a caring and neutral person who listens with compassion and without judgment cannot be underestimated. Both of these therapies are solution-based, meaning that they focus on the present and specific difficulties in our thought processes and relationships.[2]

Sit quietly with both feet on the floor and your arms by your side. Close your eyes, drop your shoulders, and inhale deeply into your abdomen. Exhale fully, and then take a few more deep breaths. Listen closely

---

[2] For more information about these therapies, please refer to Appendix One.

to the chatter in your head that is shaming you. Confront it and ask yourself if it's true. Chances are, it's not.

Let the messages go and replace them with ones that speak of care, rest, and respect for your brain. Thank your brain for the myriad of tasks it performs all day and all night. Promise that you will defend and care for it to the best of your ability.

Remember, you are a unique and wonderfully created person of immense worth. Go into this day knowing that you are one day closer to feeling like yourself again.

Day Five:
So How Did This All Start?

Information

IT HAS TAKEN ME A LONG TIME TO FIGURE THIS OUT AND MAKE peace with it, but here's how I understand the underpinnings of my depression. First of all, I was most likely born with a genetic predisposition towards it. From what my mom has told me, relatives on both sides of my family, at least two generations back, have suffered from clinical depression.

I think I had my first bout of depression when I was five. At this age, my little sister Jillie was diagnosed with leukemia—obviously, a big event in our family. This trauma shook my world dramatically and caused a neurological imbalance in my brain. Being the first imbalance of its kind, my body easily returned to health and wholeness on its own.

But later, when I was six and a half years old, Jillie died, and again my little world was rocked. The effects of her death on our family were life-lasting. My dad became an alcoholic and he raged. His marriage with my mother became very strained. Despite this, my home environment wasn't always awful; it was wonderful, fun, and loving as well.

In my teens, I became involved in competitive diving at an international level, and I had a loving but unpredictable and abusive coach.

Unfortunately, the nature of these two ongoing and unpredictable environments was extremely stressful and wreaked havoc on my internal biology. The secretion of hormones meant for temporary fight-or-flight responses became chronic, and over time their presence in my bloodstream depleted my brain's ability to correct the imbalance and return to health.

My depressive episodes became more frequent and less managed by my own natural processes. In my mid-twenties, I experienced moderate postpartum depression twice, and by my early thirties depression was a constant companion.

Although I know this now, it wasn't until I was forty that I was actually diagnosed with a Major Mood Disorder. More accurately, it wasn't until I was forty, and my kids were older and somewhat independent, that I had the courage to admit to myself and my doctor how terrible I actually felt. Hearing the truth, my doctor was able to make a diagnosis.

So this genetic predisposition to depression and the continuation of traumatic events caused me to develop a disorder in the way my neurotransmitters functioned. Therefore, I needed to supplement my body's supply with medication. I fought this, and I fought it hard—for three years. I didn't want to go on medication, and by the time I actually stayed on them I was very sick and it took longer and longer for the medication to work.

So this genetic predisposition to depression and the continuation of traumatic events caused me to develop a disorder in the way my neurotransmitters functioned.

Many years later, I continue to be monitored regularly for mood changes and am presently on several medications.

Recently I have enjoyed a whole year of stability. What a gift it is to experience the near-normalcy that others live with daily! But it's an ongoing challenge with many ups and downs, demands and limitations. Of course, the light in my life is brighter and warmer because of my knowledge of the fearful darkness. And God has been there through it all—dimly, brilliantly, silently, wildly.

Depression is a valid neurological disease that is not your fault. There are biological reasons you are feeling badly, and they are not your fault either. It is a brave thing to admit that you need help and ask for it. Place your hand on your heart and rest for a moment; take good care of yourself today.

Day Six:
Is God Allowing My Suffering?

Suffering / Comfort

THERE ARE MANY THEOLOGICAL WRITINGS ABOUT SUFFERING, AND much discussion around the roots of it. The following nine statements, or maxims, adequately and succinctly express my own beliefs that underlie all the writings in this book:

1. Suffering is not God's desire for us, but occurs in the process of life.

2. Suffering is not given in order to teach us something, but through it we learn.

3. Suffering is not given to punish us, but is sometimes the consequence of poor judgment.

4. Suffering is not given to us to teach others something, but through it they may learn.

5. Suffering does not occur because our faith is weak, but through it our faith may be strengthened.

6. God does not depend on human suffering to achieve God's purposes, but through it God's purposes are sometimes achieved.

7. Suffering is not always to be avoided at all costs, but is sometimes chosen.

8. Suffering can either destroy us or add meaning to our life.

9. The will of God has more to do with how we respond to life than with how life deals with us.[3]

---

[3] Cornel Rempel, "Nine Maxims of Suffering." Date of access: March 9, 2018 (http://www.glcportland.org/cms-assets/documents/159046-782998. lent4.pdf).

Day Seven: A Psychiatric Disease, Not a Personality Flaw

Information / Comfort

IT HAS TAKEN ME DECADES TO FINALLY ACKNOWLEDGE THE SIGNS and symptoms of my depression *as depression* and quit trying to obsessively analyze them so that maybe, just maybe, they'll turn out to be something else.

After feeling lousy for months, I would often try to pull myself up and quit feeling sorry for myself. I would try to shake off the yoke of guilt and shame and scold the inner voice that was repeatedly declaring I was all alone in this world. I thought that if I could just stop ruminating about everything so much, if I could just get motivated and get out and help somebody else, I might feel better and this nightmare might end.

Well, as I discovered time and again, sometimes getting out and helping someone did help to distract me and take my mind off how I was feeling. But when I was especially ill, it more often than not exhausted me for the rest of the day, and sometimes the next. This caused me to experience even greater shame and guilt, because it's a personal ethic of mine that we should all help one another—always—especially those who have the material means to do so, which I do. I expect a lot of myself in this area.

My increased feelings of shame and guilt are more easily accepted if I understand them for what they are: the result of the distorted thought processes that accompany depression. When I feel this way, I'm not thinking clearly. These mixed-up thoughts distort my perceptions of myself and my world. It's difficult to fight the messages of my thoughts.

Over the years, I have learned the truth: I have a neuropsychiatric disease and not a personality flaw or spiritual/moral failing. And the same is true for you. This truth helps lead us to healing and wholeness.

Are you telling yourself some pretty harsh things about yourself right now? What messages are playing in your head? What thoughts go round and round, dishearteningly telling you how short you're falling and how lousy you are at everything?

Are they really true? Honestly?

Try to remember that you are a unique and wonderfully created person of immense worth. Sit as quietly as you can, drop your shoulders, and take a few deep breaths—not as deeply and perfectly as a yogi master would, just however deeply is comfortable for you. Listen to the still, small voice inside.

I pray you will hear it tell you that you are not flawed or bad or lazy; but rather that you have a disease.

If it's too smashingly loud in your head during your depression, try going for a brisk walk instead.

Be strong and courageous, going forth in the knowledge and trust that depression is a disease, not a flaw.

Week Two

Day Eight:
A Small, Manageable Task

Information

WHILE EXPERIENCING DEPRESSION, THE SHEER EFFORT IT TAKES to do anything, no matter how seemingly small, is enough to catapult me right back into bed. And for healing, that's exactly what shouldn't happen. I mean, I *think* I want to lie in bed, but it really doesn't make me feel better in the long run. Lolling around or sleeping all day just feeds my feelings of vulnerability, worthlessness, hopelessness, and fear. Not good.

Accomplishing small, manageable tasks is more effective. Making my bed, getting dressed, washing my hair, or calling a supportive friend are examples of things that I try.

If I have a bit more energy, I may open a cluttered drawer that I've been meaning to organize. Just one drawer, not the whole room. I recycle or throw away everything I've been keeping, thinking I'll use it someday even though I haven't in the past year or two. This ends up giving me a symbolic sense of control and mastery over the chaos that zooms around inside my head. If I'm feeling particularly numb inside, at least the new order of the drawer grants me some sense of ability and integrity.

Can you think of a small job that you'd like to take on today? Why don't you give it a try? Choose something that's easy to accomplish and meaningful to you, something that will make a difference but will not be taxing.

After you've completed your chosen task, do something to celebrate: sit down with a favorite cup of tea or coffee, call a friend, or put your feet up with a heartening novel, light a candle, and say, "Yay, me!" Do anything that will bring a spirit of joy your way, even if just for a tiny moment.

Remember, even though it absolutely doesn't feel like it, all will be well.

Day Nine:
The Wonders of Walking

Information

ACCOMPLISHING SMALL, MANAGEABLE TASKS IS EFFECTIVE IN gaining a sense of worth and purpose. Another effective activity is walking. I try to walk frequently, even if it's only around my home. I think it helps because, as humans, we were created to walk and our physiology gets messed up when we stop moving and become inert. I often begin to feel like a slug—not a good thing when my head feels like mud. So, one thirty-minute walk per day in the fresh air is great. Or ten minutes, three times a day is really good, too. I just need to get up and move!

This is the exact opposite of what I want to do some days. But I know that I need to fight the impulse to check out of life and into bed. I know in my heart of hearts that I need to get up and move—not to exhaust myself, but to make sure my heart is working, my blood is flowing, and the endorphins are being secreted. It's not magic, but it helps me feel better for a little while.

And when I'm trying to get through the very next minute alive, feeling better for a little while is significant.

> All blessings on you as you walk or march or plod. Go in the strength of knowing that you are adding to the existential light of the world by doing this. You are not allowing darkness to have the last say—and that is an act of great bravery.

Day Ten: A Game Plan

Information

HERE ARE SOME DOS AND DON'TS I TRY TO FOLLOW WHEN I'M SICK. Please don't be fooled into thinking I'm some pro at this. I fall short time and again. They're guidelines:

- I try to decrease my responsibilities and delegate as much as possible.

- I get out of my pajamas soon after breakfast and keep away from baggy old sweatpants and raggedy T-shirts. Although those clothes would perfectly represent how I feel, my appearance affects the way I feel about myself and I don't want it to be worse than it is already. Also, I think my appearance has an impact on the way others perceive me, and I care about what others think.[4]

- I have a bath or take a shower and wash my hair about every second day. Hydrotherapy is wonderful, so at the very least I give my face and neck a good scrub every day, and run the warm water over my hands.

- I try not to tell everyone who asks exactly how I'm *really* doing: a few trusted people are usually enough. Everyone seems to have some sort of well-intentioned advice to give, but it's confusing and too much to absorb when I take it all in.

- I aim to get out of bed at a reasonable hour every morning and make myself a good cup of coffee or tea. I have only one cup—okay, a large cup—because although caffeine wakes me up nicely, it can also increase my agitation and make it even harder to concentrate. I attempt to be conscious of sipping the hot beverage slowly, savoring the flavor and enjoying this small pleasure of the day.

---

[4] Sometimes that's unfortunate. Other times it's a good thing. In this situation, I think it's positive.

- Leaving dirty clothes on the floor really drives me nuts, because it reminds me of the mess in my head. So I try not to let clothes pile up. I also set a goal to put fresh clean sheets on the bed weekly, but good luck with that one. Just sayin', it would be nice.

- I love to have flowers by my bed, or any other object that is beautiful to me.

- I frequently wear my kick-butt black boots and/or my black vest—what I mean is, I wear things that make me feel protected, empowered, and strong. Anything that makes me feel my best, that's what I want to put on when I'm feeling my worst.

- I love giving my feet a long, warm, sudsy soak. If I'm up to it, I'll paint my nails a color that makes me smile.

- I try to be kind to myself and move towards a place of accepting where I am at the moment. And then I fight my depression with everything I've got.

- I try to take one minute, one hour, one day at a time— especially when I'm experiencing strong emotions.

- I choose to stay engaged with loved ones. Most of the time I don't feel like doing it—it just takes too much energy, energy I don't have—but if I can take a moment and a deep breath, I usually remember that in my true self I care for these people a great deal and I truly want to be in relationship with them.

• And over and over and over again, I have to remind myself not to give up: this may take a long time, but I *will* feel better.

Remember, I don't come anywhere near doing these things consistently. I just try and keep them in mind and carry them out when I remember. They're something to shoot for, and they've kept me feeling better when I do them. I hope they help you, too.[5]

> God bless you. May God's arms be wrapped around you and may you be given a huge heaping of peace. Hang in there; you can do this. In the name of the Father, Son, and Holy Spirit, may you be bold and bright and shine in your own way, in a small way, in a redeemed and perfect way today. Look for it, it will be there; in some way you will shine.

---

[5] On a good day, why don't you think up a list of things that work especially well for you?

Day Eleven:
Thoughts of Dying

Information / Suffering

OUR DOCTORS NEED TO ASK US IF WE'RE HAVING ANY SUICIDAL ideation because they care, it's their job, and it's their legal responsibility. Thoughts about dying, and desires to do so, are symptoms of depression. Talking about these desires decreases the surrounding secrecy and thereby decreases their power. It is normal to feel this way, and sharing our feelings with someone else helps to normalize them, too.

When I fantasize about my depressive wretchedness magically being taken away, I feel a faint stirring inside with the desire to live. But the distance between it and my present reality cannot be fantasized about—it is unfantasizable.

I have so often longed for my disease to be visible and acceptable to others, but I have two inherent problems around that happening. One, I can function at a very high level and thereby fool people into believing I'm fine. And two, I cannot let go of the tight rein I have on my true feelings and act how I want. The way I want to act is like a very unhappy, grumpy toddler. Acting in these ways is visible to others, but hardly acceptable.

Even more than actually wanting to die, I have wanted to hurt myself. I think this is because when a problem is physical and visible, it can be understood by the medical profession. They know how to deal with it. I have wanted to slit skin and draw blood so that I can then walk into the emergency department, show the attending staff my arm, and say, "See how I bleed? See how I need immediate attention? See this pain here? It must hurt, don't you think?"

I understand that if I were to tell the ER docs that I was convinced I could walk across six lanes of traffic and not get hurt, or carve some figures on my forearm with a knife and not feel any pain, it would sound freaky. It would be pretty difficult to know how to treat that. There's no quick fix—no easy words, x-ray, or surgery—that will bring a timely therapeutic end to my depression and its symptoms. The behaviors that sometimes accompany mental illness can freak people out. My desire to hurt myself understandably freaks my family out. Likewise yours, most probably.

> Take a deep breath
> and risk sharing
> your distress with
> a trustworthy
> individual.

Is there one person you know with whom you could share your desires to hurt yourself? I encourage you to do so. You will feel a lot less lonely, and your problems a lot smaller, if even one other person helps you to contain them. Take a deep breath and risk sharing your distress with a trustworthy individual.

Choose this person carefully. It must be someone who will respect what you have to say, who will not add more shame to your experience, and who will act as an advocate for you.[6] Make an agreement with that person that you'll tell them if you're ever going to act on your impulses. If you tell them that you have a plan for how to kill yourself, that you don't feel safe, and that it's likely you are going to act

---

[6] If you don't know anyone with whom you can confide, please phone a crisis line. If you think you cannot be alone without hurting yourself, and if you can get yourself there safely, please go to your local hospital's emergency room. If not, call 911 or your area's local emergency number.

on your plan, that person is legally bound to tell someone who is qualified to get you the help you need. You need to know that up front. If this happens, try to remember that the person you initially told is not betraying you; they are caring for you at a time when your thinking is distorted because your brain is sick.

If your brain is sick, this is not the time for you to be making huge decisions that affect your very life. Try with everything you've got inside you to trust them. Hold on, because they are going to get you help. This is scary stuff, but you deserve special care, so shore up your courage and ask for it. Do not stop until you receive it.

You can do this. It is going to be very difficult, but you can do it. Most importantly, you deserve to be cared for. And if you can't do this for yourself, then do it for your kids or your mom, your dad, or your partner— your dog or cat or best friend. Just try with all you have inside you to ask for help. Dial the number and get help.

Day Twelve:
All Tatted-Up with Grace

Grace

FOR A LONG TIME, I WAS INTERESTED IN GETTING A TATTOO ON THE underside of my wrist. I wanted a dove tattoo, as it would remind me of God's steadfastness and surety in the midst of my chaos. I surmised that a biblical image would be a creative and protective symbol, as I would be much less likely to cut God than I would myself. I hemmed and hawed over the decision for quite a few years.

One day, my nineteen-year-old daughter, Jenna, asked me why I particularly wanted a dove. I asked her if she *really* wanted to know, and she said yes, she really did want to know. So I took a few deep breaths, asked for divine leading, and told her my reasons.

"Wow!" was her response.

And then she asked me if she, too, could get one as a symbol of her support—our sisterhood, so to speak.

Well, it so happened that two weeks later I chickened out of a full-fledged dove, but each of us got a tattoo of an olive branch on the underside of our wrist. A few days after completion, one could still tell what Jenna's tattoo was because she had the skin of a teenager—taut and full of elasticity. This kept the shape of the branch even after the swelling went down. Mine? Well, as soon as the swelling decreased, so did the outline of the branch. My tattoo ended up looking like a green blob smudged with red dots!

Hmmmm, so much for dramatic effect.

Many years later, I now have a full-fledged dove tattoo with a very discernible olive branch in its mouth which has indeed prevented me from hurting myself. There is something fundamentally wrong with cutting an icon, something that lifts our eyes to something greater than ourselves. When I was very sick, my mom placed a kiss upon my dove and caressed it with tender care. My stoic German mother-in-law held my hand and told me I had done a good thing. Blessed benedictions.

In our essential being, our heads don't droop in shame and our names aren't Depression or Mood Disorder. They are Beloved and Worthy and Precious. Every one of us. You matter, and your absence would be so very sorely noted. Hang in there. Things will get better. I know everything inside of you says differently, but in fact, it could even be tomorrow.

Day Thirteen:
The State of Your States

Information

WHEN I AM WELL AND REALIZE WHAT A CALM MIND FEELS LIKE, and what it allows me to do, I grimace to recall my attempts at meditation during a depressive episode. It's so ludicrous to think I expected myself to lie peacefully and chant the "ohms," breathe deeply, and be fully in the present moment. I have to laugh at myself.

Well, I try to laugh. I *should* laugh. Okay, so I'm not quite there yet.

When I'm in a depressive episode, I'm even harder on myself than usual. Exactly when I should be giving myself a million breaks, I expect a genius level of life management brilliance. Where do these illogical thoughts and expectations come from?

One explanation is something called state-dependent memory. It's just what it sounds like: when we're in the vulnerable state of a depressive episode, our brains recall other vulnerable states during our lives and bring up all the "files" associated with those times.

For example, I often feel six years old and experience the anxiety, powerlessness, and abandonment I felt when my little sister died, as if it were happening all over again. I hear the same messages and believe the same distorted thoughts about the world and myself despite the many years that have passed, and the hours of psychotherapy.[7]

> You are not your disease.
> You are still you
> —wonderful you.

Finally, during an appointment with my neuropsychiatrist, I found the appropriate words to explain my experience. When my doctor subsequently explained state-dependent memory, its truth kerplunked into place, settling deeply

---

[7] Coming to this realization horrified me. I was a counsellor and began doubting the whole efficacy of therapy, and of my life's work. What good was counselling if it just blasted open wounds and I kept returning to the beginning with no closure?

within. I felt cheered on by being understood and being given a name for the state I was experiencing.

Since then, this theory has served as a helpful clue that calls attention to my slipping mood. When all my past psychological issues seem right on the surface and I feel like throwing a little kid temper tantrum when I don't get my own way, I know it's time to check in with myself, my mood, and my good doctor.

Be strong and courageous, and remember that you have a valid neurological imbalance. You deserve time to rest and restore the levels of neurotransmitters that your amazing brain needs in order to function optimally.

You may feel very young during this time, so take very good care of yourself. Even though you don't always feel like it, try and act your age when you're around others, especially family; throw the temper tantrums when you're alone. This will pass, one day at a time.

Be strong in heart and spirit, and keep your integrity as much as you possibly can. You are not your disease. You are still you—wonderful you.

Day Fourteen:
Whisper to Me of Who I Truly Am

Grace

TODAY MARKS THE END OF THE FIRST TWO WEEKS OF YOUR JOUR-
ney. Congratulations! You have courageously made it this
far! Right now, drive all negative messages from your mind,
thoughts like "Yeah, big deal, two weeks and I still feel like
crap" or "Two weeks and there's six to go. I can't make it, I'm
a loser. I'll never get through the next six."

Perhaps you *do* feel a bit better. Perhaps it's not *so*
difficult to get up in the morning. Perhaps it's a little easier
to choose what you'll wear for the day. Celebrate these little
changes, even the teeny ones. Don't be hard on yourself. This

is a process, sometimes a long one. But you will get there. You can do it.

I've written a prayer for you to use today if you'd like. I hope it reflects some of the things you wish to express to God. If it doesn't, please don't pray it. That's okay, too.

O good and gracious Lord, You who are Truth and Mercy and Great Love, live within me today. Open my eyes, unstop my ears, be my thinking, and gently bring me back to You when I leave You today, for surely I will. Bind my heart to Yours. May Your joy be that which I pursue and that which is my strength. Speak into my mutterings. Help me to surrender all my anxieties and dearly beloved ones into Your care. Take from me false illusions of who I am. Whisper to me of who I truly am in Your constant, answering love. Deliver me from darkness. May my life be for Your glory and for Your name's sake. Amen.

Week Three

Day Fifteen: All the Courage
You Have Ever Had to Muster

Suffering

Courage is the most important of all the virtues, because without courage you can't practice any other virtue consistently. (You can practice any virtue erratically, but nothing consistently without courage.[8]

—Maya Angelou

LIFE IS TRULY FULL OF IRONY. ONE WOULD THINK THAT WHEN OUR family arrived at a place in life when our son was married

---

[8] Maya Angelou, "Maya Angelou Quotes," *BrainyQuote*. Date of access: March 9, 2018 (https://www.brainyquote.com/quotes/maya_angelou_120859).

and our daughter was baptized and well launched into young adulthood that I would begin to feel healthier due to a lessening of stress and responsibilities. Right?

Wrong.

What reaching this milestone did was give me permission to let go and let my chronic depression have its way—or have its voice. It meant that I finally listened frightfully but respectfully to its voice and sought to respond appropriately. It was me who needed tending to, and the empty nest my husband and I now inhabited opened a space into which I could fall. All my grey blahness, oppressive lethargy, and electric irritability tumbled out and right into a room on the psychiatric ward. My need for safety from self-harm, and my intense need for respite, outweighed my need to protect my family and myself from how desperate I truly felt.

I never, ever thought I would go to the psych ward, but there I was. I was scared spitless and deafeningly alone, but primarily I felt deeply relieved to be there. I shed responsibility for everything and everyone like a snake sheds its skin.

And then I slept. And slept. And slept some more. I made no phone calls and took no phone calls. No visitors were allowed, other than my husband. It was weird, but it was wonderful: I felt protected and hidden away, and I could just concentrate on getting better, not on being Susie Sunshine.

Have you found yourself stoically enduring the past weeks or months? I encourage you to seek out support of some kind from a safe and nonjudgmental person or group. Take a deep breath and let them know as much as you can about how you truly feel.

May you feel yourself in the safe arms of an angel.

Are you hanging onto a thin and frayed rope, nearing your end? Know that angels are under and over you, to your right and to your left. Angels of mercy go before you and are behind you.

I hope you can trust this and rest a little more easily today. I hope you can trust this, not what your distorted thoughts would have you believe. I hope that you have the faith to believe that you will not always feel this bad and that you will reach out for help. It may require all the courage you've ever had to muster, for indeed it is a brave thing to do.

Let your partner or your friend, your mother or father, the taxi cab driver, your priest, rabbi, or whomever... let them get you some help. And may you feel a deep inner peace as you have never felt before. You are not alone; you can do this. You are a brave and strong person.

Day Sixteen: Acting on Your Principles Rather than on Your Feelings

Information / Grace

May you know serenity when you are called to enter the house of suffering. May a window of light always surprise you.[9]

—Father John O'Donahue

MENTAL ILLNESS CAN SCORCH THE LIFE OUT OF A PERSON'S primary relationships, charring all the tenderness and care therein. If left unchecked, depression can wrench apart even

---

[9] Father John O'Donahue, *To Bless the Space Between Us* (New York, NY: Doubleday, 2008), 124.

the strongest of unions. A person with mental illness must choose again and again to reconnect with loved ones.

During times like this, I find that it helps to act on my principles rather than on my feelings. In other words, I ask myself what's important to me about my relationships, about how we treat one another and speak to one another, and then I try and act on that, not on how I may be feeling. How I feel when I'm depressed is all too often like a three-year-old who's just had her favorite toy stolen by a playground bully.

During a depressive episode, my thoughts are distorted, so my associated feelings are, too. I'm often confused as to what's really going on. Therefore, I need to return often to what I know to be true for myself and how I want to live my life. I need to remember what I know to be true and not base my life on the false messages that may be running through my head.

For example, when I'm not well I firmly believe that I have to do everything for my husband, that I must earn his love or he will be angered with me and leave. The truth is that he may get justifiably angry with something, but he's not going to leave me. My fears of abandonment stem from my body and brain reliving childhood memories of vulnerability and lack of safety. But in truth, I'm an adult who's able to look after herself and is in no present danger.

Distorted thoughts and beliefs need to be confronted and challenged. Sometimes I need the help and guidance of a trusted and emotionally healthy person to do this. That might be my husband, friend, or counsellor. Sometimes it takes a couple of days, or even a week, to realize what's happening, but when it does I just try to make sure that I talk to somebody when I need to sort things out, when things are feeling crazy inside my head.

Talk therapy is useful in helping people to identify recurring thoughts, discuss them, and then discern whether or not they're true in the present moment. Identifying distorted thoughts is also helpful in decreasing the fear that can be perpetuated by these cognitive processes. Of the utmost importance is that major decisions—like quitting a job, leaving a partner, going on unaffordable shopping sprees, and/or moving residences—are left to another time when one's mood is stable. And it will be stable again, I promise.

I feel sad when I read back what I just wrote. This is tough stuff. I pray that you will be kind to yourself today. Can you begin by putting your hand on your heart and spending a moment there? Just sit and feel your hand upon your chest and care for yourself.

Your brain is hurting. Think of what you would say to your friend if their brain was hurting, and then say it to yourself.

Try and rest in that same care. You may feel jittery, flitzy, and uncomfortable doing this, but try not to worry about that—nobody's looking or listening.

Try to rest with your hand on your heart and care for yourself. Now drop your shoulders and breathe. If you like, thank God for this time. If you don't, that's okay, too. May all joy and peace be yours in believing.

Day Seventeen: The Tried and True Twosome—Medication and Therapy

Information

WE LIVE IN A PRIVILEGED TIME WHERE THERE ARE MANY MODES OF treatment available for different illnesses and associated psychological issues. This is true for depression. There are anti-depressants—many more now than decades ago—and psychological therapies to come alongside them. As mentioned earlier, although it's worth mentioning again, it is very important to remain on our selected medications for six to eight weeks in order to sufficiently evaluate their effectiveness.

But we can also benefit immensely from the psychological support that counselling therapies and relationships offer as they help us identify and reorganize distorted thought patterns. Cognitive behavioral therapy (CBT) is a highly recommended form of therapy for those suffering with depression. It is reality-based, focused on the client's thoughts and on finding a tangible, helpful way of redefining and rephrasing those thoughts.

Significant psychological issues may remain after your depression has diminished.[10] This is a much more beneficial time to explore them, as your brain will be calmer and less agitated. This calmer state improves your ability to engage with the psychotherapy and enhances its effectiveness.

Therapy modes that explore childhood memories may be notably difficult to embrace in the agitated or numb states of a seriously depressive episode. This can cause confusion, increasing irritation, and shame as one feels unable to properly "do" the therapy. Also, therapy is costly. But once flourishing, psychotherapy can be embraced more fully and deeper issues can be explored and healed. You may go forth even more fully grounded and alive and well!

Medication and CBT are recommended in the first stages of moderate to severe depression. After your mood has stabilized for several months, and if any psychological issues remain, you may choose to engage in therapy that focuses on

---

[10] A note on managing side effects during the eight weeks. My doctor and I managed the side effects of medications differently depending on how I felt at the time. Sometimes I was able to hang in there and tolerate them temporarily, until they diminished on their own, but there were other times when I just felt too compromised and exhausted to put in this waiting time, so we chose to discontinue the medication and try another. It's best to remain in open dialogue with your doctor and decide together what is the ideal course to take.

family systems and/or childhood experiences. Take your time finding a counsellor with whom you feel safe and comfortable. It is very important to get the right fit, so keep trying until this happens. Some counsellors will offer a free consultation, and others are able to be claimed under extended health insurance (for example, psychologists). Although it may be difficult to obtain the services of a psychiatrist who provides psychotherapy, they are usually covered by a medical services health plan.

This task may seem daunting: so many therapists, so many therapies, and you may be wondering where to start. I would suggest you sit in a comfortable chair, close your eyes, and take a few deep breaths, ensuring that your shoulders are dropped and your body relaxed. Ask God for guidance and wisdom as you seek help from professionals. Ask the Spirit to show you, nudge you towards a specific clinic and/or clinician. Trust your intuition in this and start there.

May you feel a sense of rest in your decision. Trust that your prayers have been heard and that God's intention is for you to be well cared for and for your wholeness and healing. God intends life and love and joy.

Peace be with you, now and always.

Day Eighteen: Ceaseless Choices and Dizzying Decision-Making

Information

ON THE HEELS OF YESTERDAY'S READING, THIS MIGHT SEEM LIKE A bit of a disclaimer, but hang in there: I think you'll see what I'm getting at.

There are a multitude of therapeutic options available nowadays, all screaming to get our attention, all proclaiming to be the answer to our problems—the miracle cure—if only we will fork over hundreds of dollars and dozens of hours. And we're desperate for a cure. We're in psychic pain and we understandably want out. At times we're willing to do just about anything to feel better.

There are so many choices and, believe me, I have tried many: cranial sacral therapy, vagus allergy testing, intramuscular stimulation, naturopathy, vitamins, minerals, homeopathy, massage, acupuncture, physiotherapy, chiropractic treatments, regressive childhood therapy, spiritual direction, family systems therapy, cognitive behavioral therapy, meditation, yoga, relaxation techniques, dozens of medications, and various diets. What I had hoped would work beautifully together like a masterful symphony ended up being chaotic, leaving me in a paralyzed, extremely disappointed state! I spent so much time and so many hours on the chairs and therapy tables of these many practitioners, and nothing—nothing—seemed to help, at least not for more than a few hours.[11]

What an overwhelming task it was to try out the many therapies available and discern their effectiveness. With every new attempt, I felt temporarily uplifted and thought, *Okay, this is the one! This is the one that will heal me!* Time and again, promises were given, and so few were realized.

But let's not throw out the baby with the bathwater, for there is much to be gained by a holistic approach to your care, especially during a depressive episode. My experience has taught me that the key to holistic care is that it truly is that: *whole*-istic. And if it doesn't include medical treatment, then it's not truly holistic, correct?

---

[11] In the midst of a blinding, searing migraine, I was once told by an acupuncturist that the present migraine was a good thing, as it informed her that I was "getting ready to let go of them..."

I mention this because several alternative practitioners spoke of medications as though they were unnecessary and poisonous, encouraging me to get off them as soon as possible. Therefore, I recommend professionals who desire to work alongside a team of others so that treatments are seen as complementary. Obviously, differing methodologies will take varying lengths of time to become effective, and we need to be respectful of this. It's not sufficient to try a therapy just one or two times.

> But if any product
> or treatment
> sounds too good
> to be true, it
> probably is.

Many of the therapies available are beneficial simply because they involve touch and relationship. When we're in pain, psychic pain as well as physical, we tend to tense our muscles, hunch our shoulders, and turn in on ourselves. Massage will help to relieve this tension and encourage us to uncurl ourselves, improving our circulation as our breathing becomes deeper, slower, and more regular.[12] My neuropsychiatrist

[12] It is important to note that due to severe sports injuries during my teens, which resulted in subsequent scar tissue, physical therapies such as massage and intramuscular stimulation may not have been as effective for me as they may be for others. By no means am I suggesting that these therapies are ineffective and to be avoided.

recommends getting regular hugs from people I'm close to during the day, hugs that last at least twelve seconds.

The point is to receive appropriate, regular touch and care. We are relational, social beings and need this kind of stimulation in our lives, especially when we're depressed.

It's very difficult to know for certain what we think and believe when we're depressed. Therefore, I would suggest telling a trusted person about the therapies you are considering and asking for their opinion. You don't have to agree with them, just thoughtfully consider what they have to say because they're less emotionally involved and yet care about you and want the best for you. My husband is a good sounding board off of which I frequently bounce thoughts and decisions. This helps me to sort things out and gain a more objective, less emotional perspective. The sharing also helps draw us together.

> Go forth gently and kindly with yourself. If you sit quietly and listen for the still, wise voice within, you will gain an idea of what it is you should do. Listen to your brain, neck, shoulders, and heart. What do they need for healing? What would be helpful right now?
>
> Blessings on you as you struggle to reach out and as you seek to make a decision.

You can do this! There are friends and professionals out there who can help you. After a time of discernment, take a deep breath and allow the appropriate people to help you. Blessings on you, dear one.

Day Nineteen:
Our Highest and Truest Calling

Grace

I know that love strengthens every vocation, that love is everything, that it embraces all times and all places, because it is eternal.[13]

—St. Thérèse of Lisieux

DURING A DEPRESSIVE EPISODE, I FEEL USELESS, WORTHLESS, AND unable to contribute much at all. What am I worth when I cannot give anything out to the world? When depressed, it seems as if everything that identifies me as me—the roles

[13] "I Know That Love Strengthens Every Vocation," *Society of the Little Flower*. January 26, 2018 (https://blog.littleflower.org/st-therese-daily-devotional/know-love-strengthens-every-vocation/).

that define who I uniquely am—are gone, whipped right out from under me. And without my roles, who am I?

Who am I when I can't go to work and provide for my family?

Who am I when I can't look after my children?

Who am I when I can't stand to be in a social setting?

Who am I when I can't concentrate well enough to read a book or listen to a friend?

These are tough, tough questions, ones that I wrestled with for years. I can't answer them for you, but I can share with you what I now believe.

The really good news is that the most important role any of us has is to love: love God, ourselves, and others. I am a daughter and mom, a nurse and counsellor, friend, sister, and grandma, but these are not the things that proclaim who I am. I am instead defined by my identity as a child of God. I am a daughter of the Most High God.

As Barbara Brown Taylor so profoundly states, "That is no role. That is who you most truly are. That is where your true peace and security lie."[14] Out of this truth are birthed two firm foundations for our lives:

1. No episode of depression, no matter how severe, will ever take away our position as God's beloved children.
2. Not one bit of our self-worth and purpose is dependent upon our ability to fulfill our roles. Our highest and

---

[14] Barbara Brown Taylor, *God in Pain: Teaching Sermons on Suffering* (Nashville, TN: Abingdon Press 1998), 30.

truest role is to love God and to love ourselves so that we can love others.

Herein lies another great gift of depression: the opportunity and time to learn how to do this. When we learn how to love this way, in our hearts as well as in our heads, we are freed from the oppressive chains of ego and guilt, and the treachery of purposelessness. We are freed from the overwhelming and soul-murdering beliefs of hopelessness. No matter how sick, debilitated, or wretched we feel, we are always loved and we are always free to love.

Taylor also says that "knowing your true identity can make all the difference. It can help save your life."[15] During depression, getting out of bed in the morning is an act of love. So is combing your hair, brushing your teeth, eating nutritiously, making breakfast for your child, and going for a walk. God bless your courageous act of believing that you are beloved, and God bless your acts of loving!

> *May your thoughts be still and clear, may you be assured that you have purpose and are very important, and may all of your loving be wondrously blessed!*

---

[15] Ibid.

Day Twenty:
Dying Does Not Make Perfect Sense

Suffering

> A woman who will be like a rock in a riverbed...
> shaped by the turbulence that washes over her...
> She shines with the bursting radiance of a thousand
> suns.[16]
>
> —Khaled Hosseini

A YOUNG WOMAN I KNOW ENDED HER LIFE TODAY. HER FAMILY AND
our church family are reeling and grieving this horror. In some
ways, perhaps many ways, I understand her actions; my wrist

---

[16] Khaled Hosseini, *A Thousand Splendid Suns* (New York, NY: Penguin Books, 2007), 401.

tattoo is symbolic of this. And yet I sat in church this morning, beautifully pressed and turned out with just the right clothes, the right makeup, the right appearance. No one would have guessed that I have a tattoo, and that I have a tattoo so that I don't hurt myself when my internal pain becomes so intense that my only desire is to somehow get it outside of myself.

I wondered why I was sitting there in church, and she was not. What makes the difference between her depression and mine? Her death and my present steady breath?

I don't know.

You are a valuable
and cherished
person who would
be sorely missed
and grieved.

I do know that this is the horrific potential of the distorted thought processes of mental illness. It's so overwhelming and pervasive that even people like myself, who outwardly have it all together, still want to carve themselves up, to scar themselves. People with moderate to severe depression have stated that dying just makes perfect sense. They calmly report believing that their loved ones would truly be better off without them.

No one will be better off without you. You are a valuable and cherished person who would be sorely missed and grieved. And you have more to contribute to life than you believe you do. I know you don't feel that way, but do everything in your power to think that way. Your smile is worth everything to those who love you. And if there's no way you can smile right now, know that your presence in their lives is enough.

Day Twenty-One:
Honoring Three-Week Cracks of Light

Grace

FIND A CANDLE OF ANY SIZE AND ANCHOR IT ON YOUR FAVORITE plate. Light it in honor of all that is light and goodness. Light it in honor of you, a beloved child whose pain will be redeemed as you survive and go forth to comfort others. Light it in honor of having come through the past three weeks in the best ways you could.

Well done!

Try, with all that is in you, to relinquish your grasp upon that which you are attempting to control. Breathe into the hope that all will be well. This, too, will pass. Be gentle with yourself and others. And so it is. Amen.

Week Four

Day Twenty-Two:
Where Did That Thought Come From?

Information

SO WHAT ABOUT THESE DISTORTED THOUGHTS I'VE BEEN mentioning? What are they and what do they look like? What can we do about them?

During an episode of depression, my brain's circuits get all mumbo-jumbo and my thoughts get weird. For instance, I'm really good at jumping to conclusions: I think I know what others are thinking, and I think I can predict the future. Amazing, eh?

I also do pretty well with disqualifying everything positive in my life. You know, everything's lousy and nothing's good.

This is called filtering. The real corker is my command of the shoulds, oughts, and musts. I'm a master! "I should be cleaning the house from top to bottom!" "I should be at work today. I've got three meetings to attend to." "I ought to be making dinner tonight. After all, I haven't done anything today."

Here are some other examples of distorted thinking, or depressive thinking:

- perfectionism
- all-or-nothing thinking
- black-and-white thinking
- catastrophizing
- labelling
- blaming
- overgeneralizing
- personalization (blaming yourself for something that wasn't completely your fault, or blaming others when something was your fault)

Depressive thinking can easily become a habit, further decreasing self-esteem as it fills your mind with harsh self-criticism. It's really hard then not to become sad, discouraged, and frustrated with the ongoing frenetic tension of these thoughts. Unfortunately, this suffering often leads to withdrawal from others, isolation, and a decrease in activities and engagement with life. If it's ongoing, it can lead to some people shutting down completely and becoming numb to outside and inside stimuli.

So what can we do to manage depressive thinking and gain some sense of control?[17]

Well, the first step is to start paying attention to our thoughts and recording them, especially when our mood takes a dip. A good question to ask is, "What was going through my mind just then?" By writing down our thoughts, we can begin to recognize patterns in our thinking. As we name our thoughts, we gain a sense of mastery over them and head in a new, more positive direction.

For example, maybe you'll recognize after a while that you often call yourself names or label things you've done as stupid or idiotic. You then are aware of this habit and can catch yourself and stop, choosing to rename yourself and the things you do in a positive manner.

As you become aware of your depressive thinking, try not to judge yourself. Be gentle and remind yourself that you're thinking this way because your brain has a disease which is presently acting up. It's going to take time to get back to normal. Just knowing this will hopefully help you to recognize a depressive thought and take it less seriously. Living with a major mood disorder is stressful, and I encourage you to give yourself some slack.

Once we've recognized the depressive thought for what it is, there are some steps we can take to manage it. It all has

---

[17] For further research and study on this topic, see: Dr. Elisha Goldstein, *Uncovering Happiness: Overcoming Depression with Mindfulness and Self-Compassion* (New York, NY: Atria Books, 2015).

to do with doing a reality check. How realistic is the thought I'm having? Here are a few ideas to try:

- Ask another person's opinion about the present situation.
- Ask yourself whether most people would agree with the thought you've had. If not, what would most people think?
- As yourself, "What would I say to a friend if they were in a similar situation?"
- Ask yourself, "What do I realistically think will happen if I continue to think this way? What effects do I believe it will have on myself and others?"
- Ask yourself, "How can I think more constructively and usefully about the same thing?"

Love your amazing
brain, even
though it may be
compromised right
now and needs rest
and help.

Positive and realistic thought patterns take a while to become automatic, but take heart: it doesn't take years.

Alternative ways of thinking usually become the norm after just a few weeks. It does take practice, and at times it's going to be frustrating, but it's worth it. It will help break the cycle of feeling sad and hopeless which leads to having depressive thoughts, which in turn leads to feeling even sadder and more helpless.

You can do this! Hang in there and keep trying.

When you're having thoughts that ravage you of all rest and drive you 'round the bend, please take some time to be gentle with yourself so that you can slip easily into your day.

For instance: stop. Just stop what you're thinking about and what you're doing, and go make yourself a cup of decaf tea or coffee. Don't think about it—just put your body through the motions. When it's ready, sit down at your kitchen table with this book and your cup in front of you. Take a sip, feeling the warmth of the cup on your hands and the warmth of the liquid as it travels from your mouth down into your stomach. Take another sip, lingering long enough to savor the flavor of this hot beverage. Feel it as it travels, concentrate on its passage inch by inch, and then note its settling in your abdomen.

Okay, now drop your shoulders and focus on your thoughts. Tell yourself that you have nothing—nothing—to prove today. Your purpose for today is to live within your present and temporary limitations with creativity and love. Love your amazing brain, even though it may be compromised right now and needs rest and help. Love the anxiety that fuels your ruminating like the tears of a child who needs tender care. Pour love into it all. Take lots of deep breaths and don't try to prove anything. Nothing's going anywhere. And it's all going to be okay. Love is the Lord of heaven and earth.

Day Twenty-Three:
Well-Loved and Chosen

Grace

I OFTEN FEEL LIKE I CAN'T PRAY WHEN I FEEL SO WRETCHED, AND this leads to even more despair. Anne Lamotte says in her book *Help. Thanks. Wow.* that prayer is about seeking union. She says that this is done even if we are "bitter or insane or broken"[18] and that, in fact, these are good prerequisites for engaging in a process that will help us, in the end, get it together. She adds, "Prayer is taking a chance that against all

---

[18] Anne Lamotte, *Help. Thanks. Wow.* (New York, NY: Penguin Group, 2015), 5.

odds and past history, we are loved and chosen, and do not have to get it together before we show up."[19]

Trusting this thought—that I am loved and chosen—girds me as I try each day to muster the strength to mutter or scream, "Help!" It helps me as I smile or groan my thanks, and it nudges me to crack my eyes open, even if just enough to see something or someone that causes me to whisper, "Wow." Come to think of it, just musing upon the thought that we're all loved and chosen, regardless of our thoughts and actions, is cause for a hundred thanks and wows.

The glorious, magnificent good news is that even if we can't muster any thanks on a given day or given moment, the Holy Spirit will do it for us. We can trust this because we read in Romans,

> *Likewise the Spirit helps us in our weakness; for we do not know how to pray as we ought, but that very Spirit intercedes with sighs too deep for words. And God, who searches the heart, knows what is the mind of the Spirit, because the Spirit intercedes for the saints according to the will of God.* (Romans 8:26–27)

Hundreds and hundreds of thanks be to God.

---

[19] Ibid., 6.

When you find yourself in a place where you cannot pray, ask yourself what you're expecting your prayers to be like. Eloquent? Flowing? Intercessory? Praising? Now take a deep breath and start anew. Sit still and ponder the thought that there is no right way to pray. You are seeking communion with God, and God is already present. Trust that. Trust that you are already well loved and chosen, that there is nothing more for you to do but choose to believe in that truth.

May you be protected in the light as you struggle with your darkness, so that you may come to be filled with this glorious truth: you are God's chosen and beloved one. Go forth today in the power of that bold truth!

Day Twenty-Four:
On Your Knees

Suffering / Grace

Nothing stimulates our appetite for the simple joys
of life more than the starvation caused by sadness
or desperation.[20]

—Anthon St. Maarten

I MOST OFTEN WANT TO SAY THAT DEPRESSION IS JUST SO *SAD*. THE
keenest desperation of my life is for an episode of depression
to be over. My doctor aptly describes it as that which brings
you to your knees, and that which is trauma to your soul.

[20] Anthon St. Maarten, "If we never experience..." *Quotes.net*. Date of
access: March 9, 2018 (https://www.quotes.net/quote/48471).

What takes place when I find myself on my knees? It's a humble and humbling posture, very uncomfortable for me. Things look much different from down there. "On my knees" is a pretty difficult position to retain for long; I feel small and insignificant, invisible and powerless.

Ironically, therein lies a gift of depression, and even though it's a tough and difficult gift, it's a gift nonetheless. Among the most difficult aspects of depression are the emotions, and I include numbness. They can be powerful and paralyzing. They distort thought patterns and arrest my decision-making abilities. They make my mind feel crazy, making it impossible to rest and experience silence and solitude.

So the goal is to somehow move through these emotions in a safe way and in a safe place. Why? Because the times when I've been able to do this, I've come out on the other side to some kind of ease.

For me, depression gave me the gift of time—time to look at myself and my world from a different perspective. This wasn't a bad thing after all; it sharpened my focus onto what was most important, pulling me away from the myriad of things that flew at me and fought for my attention. Because I was on my knees and unable to do the things I normally could, I found out what was most important to me, what was most important to God. This blew apart the myth that I was only worth what I could achieve and attain through my job, degrees, promotions, and kids. It led me to a deeper and surer definition of life.

When I was on my knees, my head drooped, my eyes closed, and I began to surrender. Tears came. Anger also. Frustration. Grief. Anxiety and fear. Engulfing loneliness, tremendous loss, and deep disappointment. I found, though, that if I could stay like this a while, stay with all the stuff I had feared for so long, I did indeed survive. And then, somehow, I experienced a peace, a loosening and dropping of my shoulders, a slackening of my jaws, a relaxing of the tiny muscles around my eyes and cheeks, and my body sank into the floor.

I've done it, I thought. *I've stayed with what scared me for so long.* And I thought myself very brave.

The release of emotional, and the subsequent physical, pressure opened up cranial space and allowed for the flow of life itself. It was on my knees that I began to hear whispers of worth and purpose and love. The gift of time led to the healing of many of my fears, which in turn bathed my traumatized soul with a holy balm. I thank God—gulp—that depression brought me to my knees.

> *May you be enveloped with bravery and enveloped with grace as you meet yourself anew. Try to remember to breathe deeply and uncurl your fists. Bravely relax and keep your hands open with kindness and patience, for this is a gift that takes time and much grace.*

Day Twenty-Five: May Your Deep Questions Lead to Places of Peace

Information

THIS IS A TRICKY TIME WHEN IT COMES TO NORMALCY. ON THE ONE hand, we must let it go, and on the other, we must try and retain it. We need not expect anything to be normal—not our appetite, social life, libido, workouts, sleep, concentration, or ability to make decisions. Nothing. Our major control center is compromised. Therefore, everything is affected, so please don't beat yourself up about your limited abilities.

However, in the middle of all this change, it helps to keep a regular schedule as much as possible. This is because our anxiety tends to decrease when things are predictable.[21] Above all, try to remember that this chapter in life will pass. Don't believe for a minute that this is the way life will be forevermore.

One thing that may be unusual is that you have some questions of a spiritual nature at this time, such as:

- What is life all about anyway?
- What have I been working for?
- Where does one find worth?
- Where is God in all this suffering?
- *Is* there a God?

Maybe you're asking these questions for the first time. Or maybe you've explored them within your faith paradigm before, but what you thought were once satisfying answers now seem like trite dismissals.

It is of paramount importance during a depressive episode that you steer away from making any dramatic life changes, including those that have to do with your faith. Your thought processes are distorted and you're not thinking straight. It's wiser to wait until your mood has stabilized and see how you feel and think at that time.

Having said that, what are you to do in the meantime? I would suggest therapeutic exercises such as journaling; talking with a friend, spiritual director, or chaplain; and

---

[21] Respectfully, our daily routines will ultimately be determined by the severity of the depression we experience.

reading uncomplicated material about spirituality, faith, and religion. Explore what appeals to you, ask many questions, and then ponder things for a while, writing down key points so you will remember them. Save major conclusions for a later time.

Depression offers a valuable opportunity to explore and broaden our horizons, stretching ourselves past our firmly held boundaries, often into areas we were hesitant to venture previously.

May you be watched over carefully as you explore. May your deep questions lead to places of peace, even if they don't contain set answers. May you walk boldly and confidently, knowing that a search for truth leads to freedom. May wisdom and courage mark your way.

Day Twenty-Six:
What Will You Choose to Choose?

Information / Grace

All of us know, not what is expedient, not what is going to make us popular, not what the policy is... but in truth each of us knows what is the right thing to do. And that's how I am guided.[22]

—Maya Angelou

OUR MINDS MAY BE REELING AND OUR SOULS RETCHING IN ANGUISH as we experience the darkness of depression. Conversely,

---

[22] Maya Angelou, "Dr. Maya Angelou April 4, 1928–May 28, 2014," *Women's Crisis Services of Waterloo Region*. Date of access: March 9, 2018 (https://wcswr.org/dr-maya-angelou-april-4-1928-may-28-2014/).

our minds may be silent and lifeless. Our eyes may frantically search for calm, or they may have lost sight of life and stare straight ahead, seemingly at nothing at all.

> ...we all own something that cannot be taken from us: the power to decide how we will respond to this imposed interruption in life.

Whatever our personal experience, we must remember during these times that we all own something that cannot be taken from us: the power to decide how we will respond to this imposed interruption in life.

You haven't chosen this disease, but you can choose how you will react. This means that, even though you may be feeling irritable or utterly exhausted and unable to even mutter a reply to others' questions, you can choose not to act out these feelings. Behaving well and with integrity is not being inauthentic to who you are, even though it may *feel* as if you're living a lie. Instead you're *choosing* life. When it seems as if you have absolutely no control and no choice in your life, you must remember that you always have the choice to decide how you will behave.

It's not easy. It may be the most difficult thing you will have to do, but it's the thing you must do, because it retains everyone's dignity.[23] Being depressed isn't a license to behave any which way. It's not your fault, but it's not anyone else's either.[24]

So when you feel all of three years old and want to throw a good old-fashioned temper tantrum, what can you do instead?

Here's a suggestion. Find a container into which you can place all the truths that are inside you at this time. These truths may be written or represented symbolically in one way or another. For instance, a rock might symbolize the hard lump of anger knotted in your stomach; a handful of gnarled wire may represent the crazy and crossed misfiring wires of your neurons.

What you want to do is creatively express your truth in ways that won't harm yourself or others. Your container may be a box, counsellor, journal, priest, or bag—something into which you can safely place, or throw or scream, all your feelings. Don't censor them, just honor them as important parts of you at this time and then put them away.

---

[23] If you lose your temper one time and say things you don't mean, don't worry. Just apologize and move forward.

[24] Please see Appendix Two for helpful things you can say to express your feelings and hopefully gain the understanding of important people in your life.

Remember, you are not your feelings and you are not your distorted thoughts, even though they may feel very large and inhabit the whole of you. The parts of your brain that regulate mood and thought are compromised and need time to re-establish balance once again.

> *Have compassion and love for your brain. Take good care of yourself, one step at a time. Don't take on the world right now. Your troubles are internally based and many of them, if not all, will disappear once your mood is better. You will be much more grounded and able to manage any troubles that remain when you have healed. I promise. It will happen. Hang in there.*

Day Twenty-Seven:
Holy and Beautiful

Grace

THE WORLD SHOUTS AT US ITS FALSE MESSAGES THAT WE ARE ONLY worthy when our skin is a certain wondrous smoothness, our weight within a strict range, our hair a certain thickness and shine, our wallets and muscles of a certain bulge, and our teeth a dazzling whiteness. You know those messages; we're surrounded by them every day.

But here's the thing: real life isn't about perfect teeth and mighty shows of power. Our world may love these things and spend billions of dollars to achieve them, but they don't do much to deeply transform our minds and hearts, and therefore the world as a whole. Real life for most folks is about bills, dishes, ironing, meetings, commutes, traffic, laundry, and kids' sports games. These things are monotonous, repetitive, day in/day out, the same old shtick.

I really get tired of the everyday of life, so I'm easily lured by the media's promises of newfound fame and love and success if I just do this, or if I just do that. And I'm lured even more when in the midst of a crisis, when I feel out of control, when I want things to be something other than they are. Sometimes I just want some glamour and glitz to brighten up the grey of the everyday.

So I grab the nearest glitzy magazine or roam the shopping mall for a bit, and for a while I feel better. But the buzz wears off and irritability sets in. Finally, I remember my grounding thought: to perceive all that surrounds me daily as holy and beautiful. This leads me to where I should have started, and through it I am offered hope and inspiration. Seen, truly seen, as divinely created and thereby holy, these daily minutiae can creatively get me through another minute or hour or long night.

When I allow the Spirit to reorient my heart and mind towards my Creator's work in the world, I begin to rest and be filled with wonder.[25] For example, spending even a few moments focusing on the bright green shoots of the peony bush leads me to recall God's divine plan and mystery: all this

[25] I scan Annie Dillard's *Pilgrim at Tinker Creek* (London, UK: Canterbury Press, 2011) to be reminded explicitly of the magnificent happenings at a meek little backyard creek.

growth has been occurring invisibly in my garden throughout the winter. And I am awestruck. I need this reorientation to the God-realities before me. This shift in perspective is wondrous, filling me with a new hope, so much so that my heart actually feels lighter.

God is alive and moving and creating in *all* of His creation, in you and in me and in our gardens and ponds and our crowded urban clay pots! Recreating. Redeeming. Reforming. And I want to remember this perfect order and relinquish my chaos so that it can be redeemed, then give great thanks to our great God.

May your eyes and heart be opened to see that which surrounds you as truly beautiful. Perhaps cut a flower for your bedside table or desk at work. Take a picture or draw something that has lifted your spirits today. Was it someone's phone call or simple act of kindness? Why don't you send them a note telling them how much it meant to you?

Place your hand on your heart and reflect upon the wonder of its beating contractions and relaxations. May one moment today hold a pleasant chuckle or a belly-deep laugh for you. Isn't laughter marvelous?

> Look deeply into and past your cup of coffee or tea this morning, and bring to mind all that occurred to get it to your breakfast table. Thank God for soil and sun and rain, bean and tea leaf pickers. Sip slowly and thankfully for the sheer delight of this morning ritual.
>
> Godspeed, and may God bless your remembering, reorienting, and redeeming this day.

Day Twenty-Eight:
Uncurled, Surrendering Fists

Grace/Hope

DURING EVERY RECURRING EPISODE OF DEPRESSION, IT'S terrifying for me to come into contact with my powerlessness. It's extremely difficult to sit with it long enough to acknowledge, and then accept, its reality in my life. I feel slapped over and over again with the fact that, no matter what I try and how hard I try, this disease isn't going away just because I so desperately want it to.

As so often happens when I feel powerless, I become increasingly anxious and rigid. My breathing becomes shallow and fast, and my movements stiff. My thought processes become altered and distorted. They churn rapidly and, unusual for me, I become quite judgmental. It feels as if I lose the essence of me. I try and try, and then I try again, to regain control, some sense of mastery and power over my life. But the harder and longer I try, the more exhausted and desperate I become; the more powerless and helpless I feel. I start micromanaging every aspect of my life.

Mercifully, and oh so joyfully, I have discovered that there is an inherent gift within this hamster-wheel go-around. What begins to happen, in God's good grace, is that my fists slowly uncurl and I loosen the ironclad grasp I have on my life. I get to the point where I have no more fight in me and it is at this point, at this point only, that I begin to surrender. I surrender to the truth that I'm not ultimately in control.

At the same time, however, I realize the truth that there is something I *can* control: how I respond to my present reality.[26] I slowly surrender to the truth that depression isn't my fault and it's here to stay for the time being.

But there's much I can do to help in my own healing in the meantime.[27] I'm learning to surrender my attempts to control every aspect of my life—and my family's lives, too. As the months pass, I realize that when I'm weak, I'm much more prone to release myself from the expectation of

---

[26] See Day Twenty-Four.

[27] As someone once told me, "Buts are for sitting on!" Buts can sometimes diminish the truth of the first part of the sentence in favor of the second. I neither want to diminish nor trivialize the suffering experienced by those with depression, nor infer that suffering is worthwhile because of the subsequent transformation and hope that can be a part of it.

knowing the answer to everything I'm asked. This is a lifetime myth, something that has had a strong hold on me, and it's a delight to feel its release.

I can't do all this surrendering on my own. It's all Spirit movement.

The loveliness of all this, this gift of depression, is that I'm enabled to surrender, suffused with a spirit of freeing humility. This grows with my awareness of, my at-one-ness with, the truth that much of life is mystery.

There is a beautiful gift to be had in surrendering. It's a gift unique to each person, and it's something that touches and heals at a very core level. It does so because of our vulnerability and suffering. So it's hard, sometimes unbearably hard, but it can lead to transformation and transforming hope. And hope is what keeps us living.

> I wonder what this gift will be for you? You will be gifted, that I know. Hang in there: watch and listen carefully. It will come in its own time, but it will come. You are a brave and strong soul who will make it through this chapter in your life well and with much integrity—one step and one task at a time.
>
> Do not be afraid, for My grace is sufficient for you and My strength is made perfect in weakness. God bless you.

Week Five

Day Twenty-Nine: Living the Best Possible Way with Our Emotions

Information

TAKING ONE STEP AND ONE TASK AT A TIME IS THE ANTITHESIS TO the pace our western world keeps, and it's very difficult. It's impossible to maintain a normal lifestyle when I'm depressed. Even though I'm able to rally incredible amounts of energy and succeed for a while, most often the crash is inevitable.

When I'm well, I feel grounded and overall confident, believing I can cope with what life brings. I feel grown up. When I'm clinically depressed, I feel overwhelmed with what life brings. I feel shaken to the core by my belief that I don't have what it takes to live in this vast global world.

I feel like a child who needs protection, a covering, and an advocate.

This is tricky in my relationships because if I feel like a child—a teenager, at most—what then do I bring to them? The situation is complicated even more by the fact that all the losses of my life come to the fore during depression; it's as if the "files" in my brain are opened and tossed to and fro so that nothing makes sense and everything feels chaotic.[28]

Within this tension lies a tender dance. The question is, how can I live life in the best possible way given my mental and emotional reality? After all, I cannot behave as a child and live well at the same time.

I believe it's important at these junctures not to deny my feelings but to creatively acknowledge them. By respectfully speaking my reality to myself and others, the *whump* is taken out of my sails. My "stuff" then tends not to spill over into every interaction and pollute the energy between us. My childish inclinations can be put promptly into their appropriate space as feelings, not truths.

This calls for simple statements that explain the fact that I'm feeling out of sorts and would appreciate some extra leeway for a while. Owning my feelings in a respectful and calm way helps others to stop guessing; they can relax in knowing that my pain is neither their fault nor their responsibility.[29]

---

[28] You may remember from the reading on Day Ten that this is called state-dependent memory, or state-dependent learning.
[29] See Appendix Two.

May you be given much wisdom as you seek to manage your inner turmoil and behavior. Remember that those closest to you love you, are worried about you, and want to help but don't know how. So take a deep breath and respectfully tell them!

Day Thirty:
Touching Base with the Basics Again

Information / Grace

I OFTEN WISHED THAT MODERATE TO SEVERE DEPRESSION COULD just be "therapied" away. I suppose I believed this would give me some sense of control and mastery over my life; if I did more therapy, I would figure out the reasons for the nightmare I found myself in, and then I would be able to chase away the demons forever. But recently, after six straight months of a satisfactory mood, I dive-bombed into a depressive pit. Just like that, a snap of the fingers, the dark veil descended.

I realized then how definitive the experience of depression is. It feels so unique, like nothing else in my realm of experience. I knew it within moments, felt it in my bones, and my husband saw it on my face before I even spoke it out loud. No counselling in the world would have staved off this biological descent.

This isn't to say that there isn't a very important place for counselling in the treatment of depression. Cognitive behavioral therapy is an excellent adjunct. However, it's my belief that the primary genesis of clinical depression is biological, and this biology—in the early stages of treating moderate to severe depression—is best treated medically.

> Would you struggle
> as much if you had
> to take insulin to
> treat your diabetes?

If you still find yourself deeply at odds with being on an antidepressant, ask yourself why it's acceptable to take medications for all sorts of diseases, but not to take them when it's your brain that needs help. Would you struggle as much if you had to take insulin to treat your diabetes?

When my brain chemistry settles down and my blood levels are once again at therapeutic levels, I find that many of the psychological issues that once tore at my heart and frayed my nerves no longer do so. A few may remain, and these are the ones upon which I then focus, sometimes with a counsellor and other times just with a trusted other. When I get to this place, I am again reminded of the power of neurotransmitters, hormones, synapses, dendrites, and all that other good neurological stuff... all that good stuff over which I have very little control.

> *May you wear a garland of joy today for your spirit of heaviness, and may you drink of the oil of gladness. May your heart be of good courage, for your broken and weary bones will dance again.*

Day Thirty-One:
Sassy Powerlessness!

Joy

OH, TO HAVE MY HEART QUIETED; WHAT A BALM THAT WOULD BE. What a relief it would be to have this dread pass on, melt away, and in its place sweet mercy and calm reside.

One of the gifts of depression and existential pain is how often it walks me closer to myself and to God. In my powerlessness, I am that much more inclined toward acknowledging my need for help, and in my speechlessness my ears open themselves to whispers of welcome and forgiveness and love.

If I can wait, even if for a few heartbeats, I soon know that healing is coming near. I do not know the exact time, but I can rest knowing that it *will* come. I feel strong and free to choose—to choose life, to choose light, and to choose breath… one more breath.

There you go. Take one more breath in the easiest manner it comes. Now drop your shoulders, breathe into your abdomen, and slowly exhale. Let your shoulders drop again and lift your chin ever so slightly.

No, on second thought, lift your chin up high as if you're some highfalootin' high-society ladder-climber! There! Stick your nose in the air and be your sassiest self—just for a moment while you're all alone. Feel good? Go out with that spirit and kick depression's butt today!

Day Thirty-Two:
What Makes You Uniquely You?

Information

DEPRESSION WILL MEAN DIFFERENT THINGS TO EACH OF US. Depending on factors such as age, personality, and financial situation, our responses will vary. For example, I am primarily an extrovert. I crave social interaction and warm friendships; I love good, deep discussions and lively debate every so often. I feed off the energy of others. A dull and boring day can be transformed by a simple trip to the grocery store or a quick cup of coffee with a friend if it involves some kind of meaningful connection. Also, I'm quite comfortable speaking in public, so I enjoy facilitating workshops and lectures. In other words, I like to be out there and engaged with the world.

So for someone like me, having a chronic disease such as depression is like a sick cosmic joke. It renders me speechless and mashes me into hiding. Nothing could hit me closer to the very core of my being. Hours and hours are spent at home because I feel too vulnerable to venture outside. This wreaks havoc in my soul and dries me up like a plum left out in the hot Arizona sun. I feel as dead as Ezekiel's dry bones.

Gone is any creativity or zeal for living; gone is the excited anticipation for the day ahead; gone is silliness, contentment, curiosity, eagerness, and interest. All that remains is a pervasive, invasive, numbing heaviness. I lose my self, my actual being: who I am, what makes me, me. And this me has no energy to go out and mingle, chat, engage with others, or lead any kind of workshop. All this me wants to do is curl up on the sofa and check out.

How depression affects you will depend on what makes you uniquely you. Maybe you're more of an introvert, so spending time alone during a depressive episode won't mean the same to you as it does to someone like me. Maybe you've got three kids still living at home, while I'm an empty-nester. This, obviously, will influence depression's impact on your life and your family's. Perhaps your partner is a student and you both rely on your wage, which means it's not possible for you to take time off work, while another person may have medical coverage and a supportive, understanding boss who permits them time away while they heal.

These factors play a huge part in our responses to and management of any depressive episode. Realizing how depression uniquely affects you will help to clearly explain your experience and needs to significant others.

It takes creativity and support to figure out all the possible solutions to the presenting complications. You need to enlist others to help out as much as possible, which is much easier said than done for some people. Keep remembering that this is temporary, that it won't last forever. This, too, will pass.

> God shows Ezekiel a massive valley filled with dry and dead bones... a valley of the shadow of death, of no life, no hope. God tells Ezekiel to cry out to the bones, to cry out to God's children to rise and listen to God's voice! God's children listen, and God lifts them up, puts them back together, and makes breath to enter them and they live! God's children breathe anew and are filled with the Spirit, and they know that God is Yahweh. Where there once was death, there now is new life, new hope, new energy!

The Lord Yahweh says this: "I am now going to open your graves; I shall raise you from your graves, My people, and lead you back to the soil of Israel. And you will know that I am Yahweh, when I open your graves and put my spirit in you, and you revive, and I resettle you on your own soil. Then you will know that I, Yahweh, have spoken and done this."

Hope. Life. Spirit. Reviving breath. Amen.

Day Thirty-Three: At the End of Your Rope and Being Not Afraid

Grace

> You know you cannot get well until you admit you are sick, that you cannot put your life back together again until you stop pretending it is not broken, that you cannot find your new beginning until you say out loud... that you have come to the end of your rope.[30]
>
> —Barbara Brown Taylor

I STAYED ON MY FIRST ANTIDEPRESSANT FOR A TOTAL OF THREE months. In 1994, doctors recommended that patients stay

---

[30] Taylor, *God in Pain*, 82.

on their medication at least this long, but optimally six months.

No way, I thought, *I'm getting off this dreadful thing as soon as possible.*

I felt queasy all the time. I was dizzy, anxious, and had zero libido—symptoms I blamed on the medication, not on a thing called depression.[31] What followed were three long years of unsuccessful attempts with different antidepressants—up and down, on and off, never really committed, never really paying attention to my symptoms, just begrudgingly and gruntingly plodding through life, never fully alive. Then, in 1997, I was so sick that I could no longer pretend that I was able to function. My life was broken and it was time for a new beginning. Without a shadow of doubt, I had come to the end of my rope.

Gratefully, at the end of my rope I found my husband and my doctor. I said a temporary goodbye to the clients with whom I had a counselling relationship, closed my office, and hunkered down at home. My days consisted of long walks and naps, mundane tasks such as ironing, loading and emptying the dishwasher, and making the bed. I wanted as little responsibility as possible. I had a few visitors, and only for a little while each time. Mostly I sought out solitude—experiences that weren't highly stimulating, as well as books that were interesting, well-written, and kept my attention yet weren't emotionally upsetting and draining.[32]

---

[31] I still wasn't admitting that I had depression.
[32] See Recommend Reading at the back of this book.

My husband and I explained to our kids, who were thirteen and fourteen, that my brain had a disease and it needed a rest. We assured them that we were looking after it, that there were medications for it, and that I wouldn't be working outside the home for a few months. We told them that Dad would help out with household tasks and we would appreciate their help, too. We asked them if they had any questions.

> I had to admit that
> I couldn't fix things
> on my own.

This was a huge turning point for me. I finally admitted that something was terribly wrong. I had to admit that I couldn't fix things on my own. Lord knows I had tried—psychotherapy, physiotherapy, naturopathic remedies, chiropractic treatments, and all the rest. I kept saying that I was happy with the place I was at in life, that our kids were doing well, that I was living where I wanted to, that I had finally opened a counselling office, and that my marriage was great. But then, why? Why did I feel so lousy? So utterly, completely spent?

After I participated in a class called DSM IV,[33] I came to my mental health senses. The professor was very respectful

[33] DSM (*Diagnostic and Statistical Manual of Mental Disorders*) is the text used by psychiatrists and psychologists to diagnose mental health disorders.

of the diseases involved and those who suffered from them. The safety of her posture enabled me to take an honest inventory of my experience and admit the truth of it.

As the week progressed and my truth was confirmed over and over, I felt both relieved and scared—relieved that what I had could finally be named in a way I could understand and accept, and scared because I didn't know the path that lay ahead. Safety and grace enabled me to speak truth and get the help I needed. It strikes me as so ironic that experiencing them led me to doing the hardest thing I had ever done before.

Is there something deep inside you that's longing to be named? A truth? A symptom? A fear? God's grace and inherent safety will never leave you on your own. Christ is ever-near and ever-loving. Trust in the Light of Life and surrender your truth to the One who will bathe it in everlasting love and grace. Christ gives you His peace, this peace that the world does not understand. "Do not let your hearts be troubled, and do not let them be afraid" (John 14:2).

The Holy Comforter will keep and uphold you in whatever that truth asks you to do: "I am with you always, to the end of the age" (Matthew 28:20).

Day Thirty-Four: Anger-Filled Disillusions and the Mystery that Is Life with God

Suffering / Grace

ONE SUNDAY MORNING, OUR CHURCH'S SCRIPTURE TEXT WAS Matthew 11—a tough and striking text that left me uncomfortable and sorry for the preacher who had to somehow filter through the plethora of zingers Jesus speaks out about. Along with Jesus' woes to the unrepentant cities, Matthew 11 includes the passage where John the Baptist doubts if Jesus is the one who was to come, and asks if he and the disciples should look for another.

Wait. John doubted if Jesus was the One? John, who had spent his entire life being prepared for this ministry of preparing others for the arrival of Messiah? This can't be. What had caused such disillusionment in the Baptist's mind and heart that he should question Jesus' identity after all he had seen Jesus do and say?

In her book, *God in Pain: Teaching Sermons on Suffering*, Barbara Brown Taylor aptly describes why John was disillusioned. Basically, Jesus hadn't turned out to be what John and multitudes of others had expected Him to be. All their preconceived ideas of the Messiah were abruptly and staggeringly dashed. As Taylor writes,

> [Jesus] talks more about peace and love than he does about sin and hell. He spends most of his time with spiritual weaklings and moral misfits, and he does precious little to chop up the rotten wood that John has singled out for fiery destruction. Jesus seems more interested in poking around the dead stumps looking for new growth and in throwing parties for the new shoots when he finds them, and all in all it is more than John can bear.[34]

Most of us understand all too well about disillusionment. I spent several years flooded with anger and deep disappointment that my health had betrayed me. I had visions and plans for my midlife and I wasn't prepared to be robbed of them. My anger intensified, because throughout my previous four years

---

[34] Taylor, *God in Pain*, 18.

of counselling I had eagerly anticipated the time when I would be "finished," when the heavy yoke that bound me would be lifted and I would finally have energy and zeal for life. I banked on this magical day in the future; it kept me going, gave me hope, and was a beacon toward which I ventured. I thought I had finally found a path that would lead me out of a heavy and burdened present into a light-filled and purposeful future.

Well, as I've mentioned, my bright future didn't arrive. In some ways, I felt worse than before, and from the cell of my depression's prison I groaned, moaned, and yelled out prayers to God: "Are you there anymore? Is this my life now, or am I to look somewhere else? I can't do this life, this one here. This isn't fair, God. I've worked too hard to rid my mind of its demons. You can't tell me this is it. No way!"

I thought I deserved better. I thought I should have a good life because I had worked hard exorcising all the poison, read dozens of parenting books so I wouldn't mess our kids up, and become an expert on what it meant to grow up in an alcoholic home. I knew all about shame and guilt. Looking back, I think I would have even said that I believed in my mind that God had promised me better days.

Hmm, where'd I get that from?

Disillusionment usually brings to the fore the false thoughts we have about what's true about self, others, and God. This examination carries us deeper into the mystery that is life, into the mystery that is God, and the mystery that is life with God. The deep disillusionment I felt in my mid-forties said more about my assumptions and conclusions about life than it did about any so-called truth that God had failed me.

So where had I gotten the idea that God had promised me better days? From my preconceived notion that one gets what one works for, that one can control one's destiny, that if one has suffered already, surely God won't allow more suffering to happen. And from my belief that God would reward my hard work with happiness.

Jesus answers John's question not with anger or derision, but by listing the things that were happening, the kingdom occurrences that were taking place. The lame were walking, the blind were seeing, thousands were being fed, and the poor were hearing good news of hope. If one acknowledged and recognized these things, how could one say that there was still yet another Messiah to come?

Jesus answered my screaming questions in much the same way—by pointing out kingdom occurrences. I came to see and hear Him as the Spirit opened my eyes and ears in ways that hadn't been possible for me to do by myself.

During the first few years of depression, I had been mad. I'd been mad and wanted something or someone to come up against.

So it was that the same God who angrily declared *"Woe to you, Chorazin. Woe to you, Bethsaida!"* (Matthew 11:21) was the One who stood planted on solid ground beside me in my fury. He stood there in all His gentle power while I blasted out my indignation at having been robbed of the best years of my life. He pulled up a bedside chair as I curled as far inward as I could to ward off the all-encompassing pain of a full-blown migraine. He sat and carefully waited, offering Himself to help me contain all that which was spilling forth. Never condemning or shaming, Christ also didn't offer me any easy answers or perform a miracle that took my pain away forever. But He did enter my pain. I was not alone.

All the while, the tulips and daffodils sprouted and bloomed; the towering trees in our backyard turned their brilliant oranges, reds, and yellows; Immanuel came again at Christmas; and our foreheads were anointed with Ash Wednesday dust. Feeling so full of Good Friday pain, the ever-constant, undeniable presence of our Triune God carried me into the glorious Hallelujahs and new life of Easter Sunday.[35]

All the while, Christ says, "Come to me all of you who are weary to the bone from carrying heavy burdens. In me you will find true rest. Instead of a long list of rules to weigh you down, I will give you a garland of praise for your spirit of heaviness, and my joy will be your strength."

As Taylor wrote,

---

[35] In one of her other wonderful books, *An Altar in the World*, Taylor writes of God's omnipresence, Yahweh's embodiment and manifestations in everyday life in countless ways. It opened my eyes to see God's perpetual actions in our world.

"Blessed are those
who do not let the Messiah they are expecting
blind them to the Messiah who is standing right in front of them.

Blessed are those
who keep a list of what God is doing and not only what God is not.

Blessed are those
who are not afraid to revise the hope that is in them,
pushing through their disillusionment into a place
of new and clearer vision."[36]

Amen

---

[36] Taylor, *God in Pain*, 21.

Day Thirty-Five:
Five Weeks and Hanging in There

Information / Hope

I REMEMBER GETTING TO THIS POINT IN MY RECOVERY AND wondering when this awful feeling would ever be gone. Here I was, almost five weeks into treatment, and little if any improvement had occurred. My spirits were lagging, my hope dimming, and it was hard to keep slugging on, believing in the doctor's words that things would get better. It's a drag to be at this point. So discouraging. So soul-squelching and life-draining. I asked myself how I would ever make it to eight weeks. Surely if the meds hadn't kicked in by now, they never would, right?

But then I was reminded of the one time I had started a new medication to help manage my ruminating and spinning thoughts. I seemed to have had no positive response after six weeks. At my doctor's appointment, I told him this. We went on to chat about other things, and at the end he suggested that I stay on the medication for two more weeks, just to see. If there still wasn't any change, I was to go off it myself. There would be no need to come back to see him.

Well, praise God, my life turned around during those last two weeks. The incessant buzzing in my brain settled and things were the quietest they had ever been in my life. My thoughts became more organized, information was (somewhat) filed and contained, and I was less overwhelmed by incoming stimuli. It was like a miracle. I was so grateful that my doctor had recommended staying on the medication. What a wonder! What a gift!

It is now strongly recommended that one stays on antidepressants for eight weeks for maximum effectiveness. There is up to a twenty percent increase in efficacy in the last two weeks alone!

So if you're struggling with the length of your recovery process, please take a deep breath and try to have patience. This *is* tough going. It's not easy and requires patience and hope to hang in there. It may be one of the toughest things you ever have to do.[37] Try not to drag yourself down with

---

[37] And it may be trying on our loved ones, too, as they wait and want so desperately for us to feel better.

worry over the what-ifs; you can deal with them as they arise. Stay with what's happening in the present moment and cope with it as creatively as you can.

Remember:

- Delegate as much as possible, within healthy limits.
- Decrease your responsibility for things that are too stressful.
- Get sufficient rest and eat nutritiously.
- Walk at least twenty minutes per day, preferably outside where you will be exposed to as much sunlight and greenery as possible. Research shows that both of these elements increase mood.
- Do things that are enjoyable but not taxing, like reading a book that keeps your attention but isn't stressful in its content or format.
- Bring beauty into your life. For example, a vase of flowers by your bedside, a visit to the art gallery, taking photos of people you love or things in your garden.
- Others cannot read your mind, so speak your needs clearly and succinctly.
- See a counsellor for help with this and other valuable support, such as she or he being a neutral person to listen to your frustrations, fears, sadness, etc.
- You have absolutely nothing to prove to yourself or anyone else, and especially not to God. You are loved. Period.

You are beautiful,
strong and
beautiful, because
you are enduring.

Go out from here, precious child, in the strength and boldness of knowing that you are unconditionally loved. Hold your head up high, even though it takes everything in you to do so. You are beautiful, strong and beautiful, because you are enduring. You are making it through this darkness boldly and creatively, even though it absolutely doesn't feel like it. This will end, I promise you. Some day you will see light and you will feel lighter. Hang in there.[38]

And in the strong name of Jesus, you will be well. In the strong name of Jesus, all manner of things shall be well.

---

[38] If you can't right now, call somebody—now. There's no shame in that. Get the help you need. See Appendix One.

Week Six

Day Thirty-Six: Even in the Silence of God

Suffering / Grace

If the Lord had not been my help, my soul would soon have lived in the land of silence. (Psalm 94:17)

I HAVE BEEN A WORSHIP LEADER AT OUR CHURCH FOR MORE THAN thirty years. In the past, I most always made the choice of leading a Good Friday service over an Easter Sunday one. In preparation for the scheduled service, I found that the words flowed and prayers came much more naturally for the former than the latter. I identified with suffering—it was real and alive in my life. Easter Sunday joy and jubilation? Not so much. At least, I didn't know it as intimately as I knew darkness and aloneness.

For the first decade of this ministry, I didn't know that my identification with Good Friday stemmed primarily from my illness. It was evident that I had collected many books, music scores, and pieces of art that spoke to my brain and its pain. I was deeply blessed by the preparation and delivery of these Good Friday services, of meeting and worshiping God in meaningful, holy, and creative ways. As I prepared to lead the congregation, I walked closely with God. Scripture seemed to come alive, and my prayers were natural and flowed smoothly. One might say I was on a spiritual high.

Overall, the same can be said of what occurs throughout many, if not most, of my depressive episodes: I become closer with Jesus and more intimate as I become weaker and more vulnerable. I need God more, cry out more frequently and fervently, and sit in holy silence often. This reality helps me navigate depression. It shores me up and encourages me in the thralls of hopelessness and exhaustion.

It is a perpetual Good Friday

But there is one kind of depression where things are even darker and terrorizing still, and that is the episode within which God is silent. This is the episode where I cry out as usual, but no comfort comes. I hear no "Rest your head, Sue, and be still, for all is well." I cry out as usual and I beg, but there is no "Come unto me, all you who are weary..." Nothing. It is a perpetual Good Friday, with a powerless, crucified Christ unable to climb down from his cross and do anything, a forsaken Savior left to die at the hands of mere humans. There is no penetrating light of the world, just a silent sealed tomb.

This God-silence is the worst. I can pretty well stand any other depression but this one.

Somehow I make it to Mark's gospel and a reading of the Passion Week. I read of Jesus' walk through days and nights of torment, ridicule, and excruciating pain, of His shunning betrayal by close friends. As horrific as all that must have been, I can't help but think that it wouldn't have been as bad as whatever Jesus was experiencing as he cried, *"'Eloi, Eloi, lema sabachthani?' which means, 'My God, my God, why have you abandoned me?'"* (Mark 15: 34)

It seems unfair to me. Here was the most obedient child ever, and in His greatest moment of need the great Father abandoned Him.[39] How do we make sense of this? It's a question I have no answer for—heaven knows I've tried.

How do we find peace in our depressions when our prayers for healing never seem to be answered? When the

---

[39] I understand that I'm opening a Pandora's Box with this particular text. Am I proposing that Jesus' words suggest that the Trinity broke and God abandoned Christ? Were Father, Son, and Holy Ghost actually separated for a split second? I don't know. Doubtless, there are volumes dedicated to the exegesis of this one sentence Jesus uttered. Needless to say, this is not the forum for such an undertaking, however interesting and valid and challenging that would be.

God of the New Testament miracles chooses to ignore our pleas? When we're screaming to our God who promises to never leave us, and all that seems to be heard in reply is an echoing empty blackness?

One thing we can do is look to Jesus on the Good Friday cross and see what He did. He cried out to God and endured the suffering even though he could have changed events with a simple utterance. He could have delivered Himself from torment in a flash... had He chosen.

But He didn't. He stayed the course and engaged the pain. All of it. He embraced the loneliness, the abandonment, the absolute agony, and by doing so He fully identified with the human experience.

Christ identifies with us even in the silence of God. This is not to say that we are to lie down and embrace our sufferings in an inhuman manner and pretend to be okay with what's happening to us. This is not to say that we are to welcome suffering as something that will make us more special to God, something that will make us holier or better Christians than the next person. This is not to say that our pain is something against which we cannot reel because Christians are to be pious and meek and accept all that comes our way without complaining.

Rather, I'm pointing out Christ's posture on the cross, and His choice to remain on the cross, to emphasize the fact that we have a Lord who goes all the way with us. Jesus goes all the way into the darkest of our darkness. Jesus, the Light of the world, brings light to give life where there is none. The Word made flesh allowed His flesh to be pierced so that we may live when we feel like we're dying.

> Don't try and figure
> out how to find
> God; just try and
> rest in knowing that
> God has found you.

Even though the cross appears to be a defeat over suffering, we know for a fact that it is a victory. Nothing and no one can ever separate us from the love of God (Romans 8:39), even the silence of God.

> *If you are suffering in the silence of God, in this depression's silence, take heart. Take a deep breath, as deeply into your abdomen as you can, and drop your shoulders. Just sit for a bit. Try not to analyze, assess, figure out, and problem-solve. Just sit and drop your shoulders. Don't try and figure out how to find God; just try and rest in knowing that God has found you. You are kept in perfect protection. Amen.*

Day Thirty-Seven:
God Has Not Come to a Full Stop

Grace

WORDS HAVE ALWAYS BEEN VERY IMPORTANT TO ME. I HANG ON people's words and pay close, close attention to how they're spoken through nonverbal factors like intonation and facial gestures. My husband would say I grant too much power to what he says sometimes, but I think what we say has a tremendous impact on others, for better or worse.

I come by this honestly. Family members have English degrees, and if my dad had followed his heart he probably would have been an English professor rather than a doctor.

I remember playing a game in which my siblings and I would open the fat Webster's Dictionary that lay on the pedestal in the living room, randomly point to any word, and ask my dad the meaning of it. He'd break it down into its Latin origins and, with a wry smile, proclaim the definition to our astonished faces. He wowed us over and over!

Both my mom and dad constantly corrected our grammar, never missing an opportunity to do so. That my own children so eagerly continue this habit of correction makes me both smile and groan.

Anyway, speaking English and expressing oneself eloquently was encouraged in my family, and also in the high school I attended. We were frequently required to stand in front of the class and present essays and debate our assigned position. Speaking and writing grammatically correct English became automatic and deeply engrained. I did it without a second thought. I thoroughly depended on it to usher me through socially awkward or challenging situations, and to bolster my ego when I felt anxious. I could fake it, coming across confident, even when inside I was shaking and shuddering.

But all this changed with each depressive episode. The shaking and shuddering increased to such an extent that I had to cancel public speaking engagements and opportunities to lead worship. Phone calls went unanswered. My confident voice and veneer would vanish; I seemed to have no idea of my opinions. Things became so muddled in my head that I had no idea how to defend my faith or stance on anything. I couldn't even organize my thoughts and reflect them in a coherent manner. Most distressing of all, because it was my main role, I couldn't offer comfort and kindness to others.

All of this hit at the core of my identity. No longer being able to express myself coherently through words, no longer able to connect with others through meaningful dialogue, I lost myself. Gone were long visits with friends where mutual understanding was shared. And gone were the meetings where ideas were creatively brainstormed and I gained a sense of productivity, contribution, and inclusion.

At least, this is what I thought was happening. My husband and a few other key people tried to persuade me otherwise. According to them, and contrary to my conclusions, I hadn't fallen off planet earth. Apparently life was still as it usually was, and I hadn't changed much. Sure, I was quite a bit slower and not as energetic and quick to jump up and get going, but mostly Sue was Sue. The core of me was still intact.

This was very difficult for me to believe, because inside it felt like the exact opposite was true.

What I mean to say is that when you feel like nothing is going on and you're useless and unable to do anything you used to be able to do, God is still working. When you wonder what the purpose of your life is anymore and it feels like all has come to a full stop, God is still working. God's purposes are still unfolding in your life. God is still using you to make His kingdom come to pass.

God has not come to a full stop: Yahweh is above and beyond, over and under your depression. Nothing that is of your depression is powerful enough to cause God's work in and through your life to come to a full stop. Nothing in your depression is, or ever will be, powerful enough to separate you from the love of our gracious Emmanuel.

When speaking publicly, the Apostle Paul could have used lofty and eloquent words to woo his crowds, but he held back so that the truth of the gospel, the Jesus-truth, could shine through. And if anyone needed something to attract a crowd, Paul would have because apparently he was nothing to look at: "a man of small stature, with bald head and crooked legs... with eyebrows meeting and nose somewhat hooked."[40]

I've also read that Paul suffered from depression. But just look at what Paul accomplished, what he spoke and wrote, the thousands of lives that were and continue to be transformed through his words, despite his physical and mental limitations.

I often get tied up in knots and hissy fits when I measure myself and my life's worth according to the world's values. I forget that we are:

lovers of a God who specializes in turning the world's values upside down. We are the followers of a Lord who waited tables and washed feet. We are the

---

[40] Taylor, *God in Pain*, 133.

heirs of a Spirit who has power to revive the whole creation, beginning with us, but only if we will allow it—by giving up all illusions that we know how to save ourselves and begging God, one more time, to show us how it is done.[41]

I *think* I know how to save myself, and so I keep trying to do so. I want to give this up; it's exhausting and wasteful. I want to ask God to help me let go and stop pretending that I know what's going on. I want to ask God to gently stay with me as the Spirit restores me to life and I more easefully join the Almighty's hopes and intentions for our world.

It is entirely possible that some of our proudest achievements are embarrassing to God, and some of our most dismal failures please God very much.[42]

So when I think nothing is going on because I'm too sick, I need to stand up sharply and remember that our Lord never stops acting. Yahweh is in the business of the ongoing transformation of my life and the lives of those around me. God is in the business of restoring life from death.

The only thing we can be sure of is that everything we offer up—ailing churches and prosperous

---

[41] Ibid., 135.
[42] Ibid., 136.

ones, tongue-twirling preachers and those who struggle with every word—they are all eligible for the transforming power of God, who loves nothing better than bringing the dead back to life.[43]

Your own gift might not be eloquent speech. It may be leading a business team, teaching a class, coaching volleyball, raising kids, tending a garden, or building a house. Whatever it is, when you're unable to do it to the level of perfection you demand of yourself, remember that God does not quit on you. And God does not quit *in* you.

When I'm in the grips of depression's speechlessness, I want to remember that there are other ways of speaking than with words. I want to remember that the Holy One continues to speak—even through me, even to me—safe, comforting, life-giving words of transforming love. I am not asked to be a perfect vessel, only a willing one. I am not asked to know everything, just to be willing and open. I am asked only to stay open. And I need to try and remember that it is through the cracks that the light gets in.

> Remember, our Lord continues to speak: "Do not be afraid, for I am with you always." Remember, your life continues to speak even in times of unbearable silence.

---

[43] Ibid.

Perfection is not a prerequisite to enter and belong in the Kingdom of God. Behold! It has come near and it welcomes you into its midst; you are a valuable and worthy citizen, just as you are. So shine, beloved child, shine your radiant soul into the song of life.

Put on the garment of praise for your spirit of heaviness. God's joy will be your strength alone. Remember, through it all that our Lord continues to speak: "Do not be afraid, for I am with you always." Amen.

Day Thirty-Eight: The Fear that Is Your Cross Is Also the Cross that Leads to Life

Grace/Joy

DO YOU KNOW ONE OF THE THINGS THAT HAS MADE ME ANGRIEST about having depression? It's that I work so hard at eating properly and exercising regularly and keeping my stress at a healthy level and still, *still*, I'm not physically and mentally well. I mean, when one is being super conscientious and purposeful and disciplined about all this, should there not be a natural reward of good mental and physical well-being? I mean, really, you reap what you sow, right?

But as most of us are too painfully aware, life isn't like that. We can be walking examples of near perfection, yet smooth paths don't automatically follow. Even our faith confirms this: try as we might, pray as we do, even with and through God, things don't happen and turn out as we so desperately hope. Time and time again. Even as Christians, we aren't guaranteed a picture-perfect life. In fact, Jesus urges us to take up our crosses.[44]

What is my cross? What does Jesus mean when He tells me to take up my cross and follow Him? I've often wondered about that. During Lent, I think of Christ's cross a lot, and to me the concept denotes something heavy, tremendously burdensome, very painful, and all-encompassing. It prevents free movement and easy breath; it is cumbersome, limiting, and stagnating. Crushing.

What in my life makes me feel this way?

The thought of dying? Somewhat. But not really, especially when I'm depressed.

The thought of one of my loved ones dying? Yes, of course. When I spend any time really thinking about this, I can become paralyzed by fear. But on an everyday level, I don't think it ever rules the day, directing and manipulating my thoughts and actions any more than the next guy.

The life-sucking, soul-murdering aspects of depression? The deep, dark pit of it that has me completely convinced I'll never return to the light? Ah, yes, now we've hit paydirt. This is the cross that lies heavily across my shoulders, stagnating my breath and stifling my desire. This is what envelops my

---

[44] Nothing He didn't do Himself.

brain and numbs my soul, gutting me with fear that I don't have what it takes to make it in the world out there. It's the ugly burden that stops the flow of Spirit-breath and silences the whisper of God's *"Do not be afraid; for see—I am bringing you good news of great joy"* (Luke 2:10). This is the cross of fear that cripples my surefooted gait into life's challenges, weighing me down and sucking all joy out of spontaneous responses to God's promptings.

What is that cross for you? What is the fear that plagues your dreams and stifles your joy? What is the thing from which you run, the thing that demands much of your energy day in and day out?

It's important to identify your fear, not only because it robs you of energy but because the fear that is your cross is also the fear that leads to life. In the past couple of years, I've learned to do something when the cross of fear lies heavily across my shoulders and I can barely breathe. I pause for a moment and breathe more deeply. As I do this, I focus on the Father, Son, and Holy Spirit, slowly becoming reoriented to the Trinity. As I relax this way, I'm better able to risk getting out of bed one more day, better able to risk answering the phone, better able to risk remaining connected to my husband by asking him about his work. And I might even risk going for coffee with a friend, even if it's only for half an hour.

Throughout these occurrences, life begins to sprout forth—over the coffee and biscotti, the phone and the email, I hear that I am cared for and loved. This is because I'm a beloved child of God; it's not because I've done a great job at something and fulfilled an expectation that someone else had of me.

I live this truth when a friend really wants to know how I am. I live it when a church leader asks if I can lead worship a month from now. I know this most assuredly when my husband makes dinner, once again. I know it when the tears flow while we sing during Sunday morning's worship service.

Surprise, glorious surprise! Good news of great joy! My old myths of having to work for another's acceptance and love are dashed and squelched, and I'm startled into realizing that if I was always well I wouldn't experience such love and grace in the same way.

God has been faithful and given me courage over and over. The gift of depression is that I'm learning with each episode to trust that I don't need to do something in order to belong in God's kingdom on earth, as it is in heaven. I'm learning to trust that the worker who arrived last does indeed receive the same wage as the one who arrived first. Jesus' words that the first will be last, and the last first, are slowly but surely transforming my heart.

Unfortunately, only when I come to the end of my resources do I choose to more fully turn to God and find that God is there waiting with a much better resource than me, myself. The omnipresent Spirit is the Giver of all great gifts, even the gift of my depression cross.

Come unto Me all you who are heavy burdened with crosses and I will give you rest. Do not be afraid, for My yoke is easy and My burden is light. Come to Me with the darkness of your fears, for I am the Light of the world and darkness cannot hide. Even your darkness is not dark to Me, for I am Light. Come unto Me and I will give you rest. Amen. [45]

[45] Paraphrase of Matthew 11:28-30, John 8:12 and Psalms 139:12-14

Day Thirty-Nine: Spear- and Nail-Pierced Wounds Embrace Our Bruised Hearts

Suffering / Hope

WHEN I'M OUT OF A DEPRESSIVE EPISODE FOR A NUMBER OF weeks, I'm often struck by the realization of how I had been simply surviving during it. When all of life's energy is poured into just getting by, life becomes very small and its vision myopic—I can see little beyond my tightly held, inward-looking blackness. Everything slows to a snail's pace. I recognize an "otherness" to depression, as if I live in some other realm during the months when I'm ill, and something so infiltrating and all-consuming seems to take up residency in my brain. My headspace feels occupied, almost taken over.

As mentioned before, my doctor describes depression as that which is trauma to your soul and brings you to your knees. I find this to be so true. As such, the *experience* of depression doesn't leave me when the pathology has run its course. I often feel a kind of "depression hangover," so to speak, a tender psychic bruising that stays with me for weeks after I've recovered from the physical symptoms. I do indeed feel like my soul has been traumatized.

I suppose this is because depression seems to hit at the very core of my being. It affects my mood and temperament, perception and cognition, my ability to filter, interpret, and store stimuli. In short, it affects everything to do with how I experience and evaluate life. I believe it affects who I am in a way few other diseases could. No wonder the experience of it is bound to linger awhile, even once the presenting symptoms have diminished.

After each episode of moderate to severe depression, I experience a time of grieving. Like most significant losses in life, I've ventured through these stages of grief as I let go and make peace. Each time has been different in length, but all have included a deep sense of loss, sadness, and loneliness. Every time, I feel an aching sense of being bruised all over, especially my heart. I find it difficult to describe it, maybe because it feels so very private and intimate. I don't know. Words don't come easily.

The wondrous thing that happens during this time is that our wounded, risen Christ walks into my upper room and says, "Peace be with you." Jesus' wounded hands and feet and pierced side comfort me in their imperfection and humanness; they tell me of a Savior who knows of my suffering and comes to me in and through it.

> Jesus' wounded
> hands and feet
> and pierced side
> comfort me in their
> imperfection and
> humanness.

But the Son of God's suffering is also above and beyond mine, and in His tenderness He shows me a way through mine. Christ returns in an imperfect body, continuing to identify with all of us who suffer, continuing to comfort us and be one with us until we're all made complete when the new heaven and earth are ushered in.

In the meantime, Jesus has risen! He has conquered depression and death through a love that is the greatest force of all. It is a love that says, "Peace, My child, peace be with you. Do not fear, for I am with you always, in all ways."

The Lord is your light in your fear, the stronghold of your life. Of what shall you be afraid? Though many things seem to be warring against you, may your heart not fear. Though your body may feel as if it's rising up against you, may you be confident, for the Lord will hide you in the shelter of love on the day of trouble. You will be concealed under the cover of God's tent and be set upon a rock. Your head will be lifted up above all that frightens you as you sing and make melody to the Lord.

God will hear you when you cry aloud. Yahweh will be gracious to you and answer. Believe that you shall see the goodness of the Lord in the land of the living. Wait for the Lord, be strong, and let your heart take courage. Know that God's steadfast love will be upon you, even as you hope in Christ.[46]

---

46 A paraphrase of Psalm 27 and Psalm 33:22.

Day Forty:
Songs in the Night He Giveth

Grace/Joy

O God, you are my God, I seek you, my soul thirsts for you; my flesh faints for you, as in a dry and weary land where there is no water. So I have looked upon you in the sanctuary, beholding your power and glory. Because your steadfast love is better than life, my lips will praise you... for you have been my help, and in the shadow of your wings I sing for joy. My soul clings to you; your right hand upholds me. (Psalm 63:1–3, 7–8)

OUR PASTOR, MARK, ASKED THE QUESTION TODAY, "WHEN WE FIND ourselves in overwhelming circumstances, how do we remain connected to a life-giving God?" Surely, I thought, major clinical depression is an overwhelming circumstance, so I immediately sat up straighter, quickened by the anticipation of answers to this immensely important question. I, for one, keenly wanted answers, desperately wanted answers, longed for answers.

His sermon was titled "Psalm 63 in Six Words!" And the six words were: naming, thirsting, remembering, singing, satisfied, and secure. The presentation of these six words, and their ability to help us remain connected to our life-giving God in times of overwhelming circumstances, was so helpful that I want to pass it on to you.

This can be seen as a simple exercise you can employ when you're feeling distraught and disconnected spiritually, a way to guide you back toward home when your illness has muddied up the path and your footsteps are unsure.

First of all, **naming**. You name the presence of God, acknowledging the reality of the divine in your life. As Psalm 63:1 says, *"O God, you are my God."* God is already with you, God hasn't left you, and you simply need to bring this into consciousness by stating it as fact.

Secondly, acknowledge that you are **thirsting**, that you want to not only know your Triune God in your head but in your body—holistically, fully, completely infused by the Holy Spirit, intimately walking with and through our Lord.

Next, spend a bit of time **remembering** the presence

of God in times past. In doing so, you may remember the trauma in your past, but concentrate on the parts within that story that speak to the unmistakable presence of God.

For example, my dad was diagnosed with Alzheimer's about a year and a half before he died. In the last weeks, he had a few falls and it was impossible for my mom to lift him by herself, necessitating the help of others. One time this happened in the middle of the night.

Although the circumstances surrounding the end of his life were very upsetting to all of us, they were much more exaggerated for me as I was in the middle of a major depressive episode. After a particularly difficult and desperate day, a very dark one, I awoke in the middle of a deep sleep and remembered a dream I'd had. The scene was my parents' bedroom. My mom was standing by the bedroom door, agitated, wringing her hands and looking down at my dad's body on the carpeted floor in a fetal position. Obviously, he had fallen again. But soon thereafter, a fluid, semi-transparent Christ-like figure bent down on one knee and gently lifted him off the floor and placed him back into bed. This gesture was done with so much tenderness and love that tears flooded my face in thanks to our Savior. The amount of love He had for my dad was palpable: it was an actual entity in the room taking up space.

I remember painful events from my past, such as my father dying a terror-filled death, as being bathed in grace notes of Jesus' love.

The fourth word is **singing**, and it's related to the fifth and sixth words, **satisfied** and **security.** Mark asked us what song we sing when we're overwhelmed, and if we don't have one he suggested that we find one. I have many significant and favorite songs, but the most meaningful ones are "My Life Flows On" and "My Hope Is Built on Nothing Less."

What though my joys and comforts die?
I know my Savior liveth.
What though the darkness gather round?
Songs in the night he giveth.
No storm can shake my inmost calm
While to that Rock I'm clinging.
Since love is Lord of heaven and earth,
How can I keep from singing?[47]

His oath, His covenant, His blood,
Support me in the whelming flood;
When all around my soul gives way,
He then is all my hope and stay.
On Christ, the solid rock, I stand;
All other ground is sinking sand,
All other ground is sinking sand.[48]

My anxious questing is satisfied in knowing that—no matter what, no matter how dark—love *is* the Lord of heaven

---

47 Robert Lowry, "My Life Flows On," 1869.
48 Edward Mote, "My Hope Is Built on Nothing Less," 1834.

and earth. Love is the moving and living and breathing Light in the world. It is the truth in sickness and in health, for better or for worse, in life and in death. And love is the ultimate victor. In the meantime, the Rock of Christ is that upon which I stand, or fall, lie prostrate, or cling to: it is unmovable, unshakable, dependable, and sure. I am secure in this knowing and I rest.

Now I'm resting, sweetly resting,
In the cleft once made for me.
Jesus, blessed Rock of Ages,
I will hide myself in Thee.[49]

Take a deep breath, down into your abdomen,
 and exhale as slowly as you can.
Drop your shoulders towards your hips and
rest.
Pretend your hips are the base of a mountain
 and reflect upon how strong you are,
 how grounded and sure.
In this posture, begin to think about God
and the names you use —
 Comforter, Almighty, Creator . . .
How does God's presence feel in your body?
Where do you feel God's presence?
How about Jesus' presence?

[49] Mary D. James, "In the Rifted Rock I'm Resting," 1878.

And the Holy Spirit's?
How are you thirsting for God?
Name your desires and know that Jesus is
beside you in each & every one.
   He receives them with care and holds them
tenderly.
Feel your hips on the chair; feel that
mountain base;
   you are strongly and securely grounded.
In this strong posture,
   think if there is something that is
   overwhelming you
   at the present time.
What song do you sing into that uneasiness?
   Perhaps write out the lyrics you find
   especially helpful
   and come back to them over the course of
the day.
   Let the truths and promises of the words
fill you with the
   comfort and joy that come from our good God.
Bathe your unease with the love of the
Father,
   the redemption of Jesus the Son,
   and the life-healing breath of the Holy
Spirit.

Day Forty-One:
Lifted Up Above All that Terrifies You

Suffering / Hope

DO NOT BE AFRAID, MY FRIEND, BECAUSE THE LORD IS YOUR LIGHT and your salvation. Yahweh is the stronghold of your life. All that which seems to be against you will fade away and your heart will be made strong. You will be confident even when it feels as if war is raging inside you.

May the Spirit calm you so that you may meet God and behold the beauty within. Your head will be lifted above all that terrifies you. As you feel joy, you will sing. Yes, you will sing!

In God's grace, God hears when you cry aloud and you will be answered. Jehovah's face will not be hidden as you seek it, and you will not be turned away from the God who has been your help and salvation. You do not anger your Lord, and you will never be forsaken, even if your mother and father do so.

God will teach you the ways of goodness and lead you on a level path, away from those of adversity and violence. You will see the goodness of the Lord in the land of the living.

As you wait for the Lord, you will be strong. Your heart will be full of courage as you wait. Courage, courage, and more courage!

Day Forty-Two:
The World's Standards or God's?

Comfort

...we who have taken refuge might be strongly encouraged to seize the hope set before us. We have this hope, a sure and steadfast anchor of the soul, a hope that enters the inner shrine behind the curtain, where Jesus, a forerunner on our behalf, has entered, having become a high priest forever...
(Hebrews 6:18–20)

ARE YOU SLOUCHING TODAY? TIRED AND WEARY OF THIS CLIMB? Are you discouraged from pulling yourself up every day, making the best of your circumstances, keepin' the old chin up? Are you feeling shameful that for five weeks you seem to have hardly done anything except keep your head above water? Are you feeling useless because it's still a fight to even get the dishes done each day?

Let me ask you the question that's most important: are you measuring your worth by the world's definitions or God's?

I find that the answer has a direct correlation to how much hope I feel. When my mind is full of *shoulds* and I'm not measuring up to any of them, it's a big clue that I've allowed the world's messages to take up residence. It's not a difficult thing to do. After all, they're blaring at us from everywhere. You know the ones: be beautiful, be thin, be rich, be on top of things at all times, be intelligent, fix everything that isn't top-notch inside and out, have every corner of your house organized, be assertive, have the best exercise regimen, etc. When I'm in this place, I don't get anywhere but down and hopeless and dark. And I feel very unsettled, wobbly, and disoriented. Nothing feels secure.

I guess that's no surprise. When we look at ourselves from the world's perspective, we're distancing ourselves from God's. We are not at home.

Getting reoriented can be tricky, especially when we're vulnerable and suggestible. I find it helpful not to expect a lengthy time of great meditation or prayer. I try for meaningful moments. I sit down, focus on a few breaths, and say a few words, trusting that Christ is neither measuring nor judging them, but simply delighting in our communion. I ask my Creator to reset my mind by bringing to it images of goodness and grace, love and mercy. And then I just sit as silently as I can for however long I can. Sometimes it's only three seconds! Then I try and leave it at that, trusting that God is going to continue working in my mind.

Sometimes I turn to the psalms. These can be especially helpful in reorienting my thoughts. Other texts are those that have to do with Jesus' interactions with the marginalized. Particularly poignant for me are the stories that have to do with women on the fringe.[50] Read the parable of the prodigal son—or even better, think of it from the perspective of the prodigal father—and become familiar with just how radical God's preposterous love is.[51]

One of my very favorite texts comes from Hebrews 6, quoted at the beginning of today's reading. We have a hope in Christ that is a sure and steadfast anchor. A sure and steadfast anchor! Think of it: in the first place, hope of any kind sounds pretty good, and a hope that steadfastly anchors us offers untold blessings of comfort. It hints at a trustworthiness to which we can return time and again. It also speaks of a bedrockness, a grounded trustworthiness that will keep us secure.

---

[50] Weren't all women on the fringe in Jesus' day?

[51] I'm sure you have your own favorite texts. It's helpful to have a list of them at the ready so they're easily accessible.

Ahh, I'm feeling more defined already. My backbone is straighter and stronger.

The writer of Hebrews tells us that Jesus, as our hope, enters the inner shrine behind the curtain. In traditional Jewish faith, this is known as the Holy of Holies, where the High Priest would go once a year to make atonement for all sins. But in the New Testament, we learn that Jesus made atonement once and for all. Thus, this venture into the Holy of Holies is no longer required.

The Hebrew imagery reflects Jesus' passage into the one true sanctuary of the loving Father. As believers in him, we are anchored there, in the very presence of our merciful God; we remain there forever, securely connected to Father, Son, and Holy Ghost through all the winds, storms, and thunder that may come.

Author Tom Wright put it this way:

> We are not promised that there won't be any storms; indeed, the provision of a secure anchor implies that there will be. What we are promised is that we will be kept safe.[52]

Christ suffered the mockery, the lashings, the rejections, and the silence of God so that He could go before us into the Holy of Holies and there sit beside our Father and say, "It is finished." What was finished? All that it took for us to forever

---

[52] Tom Wright, *Hebrews for Everyone* (London, UK: SPCK, 2003), 66.

remain connected and safe with our loving Lord. Is this not amazing love? Is this not grace unbounded?

What other kind of love is needed to see us through our depressive episode? As the objects of such love, what does it say about our worth?

What is it like for you to think of yourself as so loved? Sit quietly and let that sink in for a moment. As sure as the day began this morning, God's presence and love are there for you today. Go forth in the boldness of that truth.

Get those shoulders back and that chin up. Be cheeky if you want to; you don't have to slouch, you know. You have a strong metal cable anchoring you to God and nothing will sever it—ever. You are meant to conquer all the things that are holding you down, and with time you will. Claim that and go forth! Amen!

Week Seven

Day Forty-Three:
Spirit Whisperings of Healthful Change

Grace

I'M SITTING IN MY STUDIO WAITING FOR INSPIRATION TO COME, waiting for some great idea. In the meantime, the rain falls, adding to the huge puddle that has gathered in the corner of the garden by the fence. Finches play happily at its edge, sipping the cool water, jiggling their bodies to shake it off after their plunging baths. They're well fed, too, as my husband has just filled the birdfeeder with organic, already-shelled seed. Wow, a bird's paradise! The flickers will come later in the afternoon. My spirit marvels once again at the orange undersides of their wings as they dart to and fro from pine tree limbs back to the feeder.

I recall how this backyard of ours has anchored me in times of grey despair, especially in the spring, as it is now. Bright green sprouts, almost neon in sheen, have pushed through the rain-soaked soil to show their hope and announce the promise of my favorite season's arrival. The soft pink of the hellebores is calming, their prettiness making me smile a gentle smile.

We have a single, simple camellia bud adorning our kitchen table, and its mere presence seems to be some kind of bold proclamation, even though the flower is small. It speaks of something bigger than itself or even ourselves.

Hmmm, my soul purrs. *Sweetness. Gentleness.*

Something is well out there in our garden. The skies may be grey and foreboding, but the green grass is brilliant and rich, and it drinks well from those skies. The daffodils' sunny faces are just beginning to shine and birdsong is everywhere.

I love our backyard with its different gardens: roses, rhododendrons, vegetables, lilacs, ferns, peonies, and hydrangeas, all stunningly beautiful. I marvel at their brilliance every summer, as if seeing it for the first time.

But around late August, both my husband and I get tired from all the upkeep. Our energies begin to wane just like the hydrangeas. Especially mine.

So this summer, we've made a decision to downsize. We're going to move to a much smaller living space. This has been a pretty difficult decision for my husband; he doesn't much want to do this, but he's choosing to do it to support me. I'm thankful for that, as I find our home too big to look after.

Two weeks ago, our son and daughter-in-law called from the U.K. to announce the safe and healthy arrival of their baby girl, our second granddaughter. More new life! More hope and dreams! Oh, the joy and sweetness of it! The innocence and newness and fresh start! Shouts of joy and prayers of gratitude rang out across the seas!

A week after that, our son called again, this time his voice shaking as a torrent of tears fell. He felt totally overwhelmed with all the worries and powerlessness that go along with being a first-time parent. And he felt guilt and shame for feeling that way. He and his wife were experiencing a loss of control, a loss of being just husband and wife with the time to do things their way and when they wanted to do them.

So, of course, we as family have been rallying around them ever since, sending our love, prayers, and well wishes. Wish as I might, I can't do it for them. Only they can go through this and try to trust our words that it does get better, that it will pass.

Life, eh? My garden both delights me and exhausts me. My big house opens up so many opportunities and overwhelms me with so many things to do. I love the energy and zeal for life of my two-year-old granddaughter, and at the same time I'm exhausted by the emotional and physical investments I choose to make. I love church and my church family, but sometimes the energy it takes to care for people there and the politics are too much to manage.

How do we do life when life also includes a mental health issue? My disease has quite a lot to do with my decision to have significant parts of my life be smaller. I can't do it all on such a grand scale. For instance, hosting family dinners often leaves me feeling very drained. At the present time, we live communally with our daughter, son-in-law, and their little girl. They live in an apartment upstairs. Because the downstairs where we live is much bigger, we host all the communal dinners and celebrations at our place. Well, I'm at the time in my life and my disease process when I would like to be in the apartment, so to speak, and come downstairs to have dinner in my children's place. The natural time of switching roles has come somewhat earlier for us because of my health limitations.

This has been no small issue to process in our marriage. But as we've recognized, this move may only be for a season. We don't know. We're going to try it and find out. Right now, we don't have enough information to know if being in a smaller place will be helpful, but in a year or so we will know.

So here I still sit, looking out my studio windows at my rain-soaked backyard, aware that it brings me both joy and exhaustion. I want to hold that truth before myself and God always, with much thanks.

What do you think you need to do at the present time to help manage your health? Is there something you need to communicate to friends or family that will help you live more fully, and help you thrive within the realities of your disease?

May you be blessed with eyes to see the dance of the birds and the shine of the tulip's upturned face, the shout of the broom bush and the radiance of the forsythia's yellow. May you hear of Spirit whisperings that tell of healthful change so that you may thrive in your days and slumber well in your nights. May you be filled with lion-hearted courage to walk these new paths, and venture boldly as you are filled with the Spirit power of Emmanuel. Emmanuel, God with us! Yes, Emmanuel: praise be to God!

Day Forty-Four:
Cosmos in the Midst of Chaos

Grace/Joy

BEFORE READING TODAY, LISTEN TO THE SONG "SONGBIRD" BY Fleetwood Mac. There is a theology to the song, a theology that reflects and proclaims the ongoing nature of God's cosmos even when we aren't able to participate in the world around us.

God's divine ordering of our world continues in the midst of anything we may be experiencing at any given time. Even when we're at our darkest, the songbird involuntarily continues to sing its song—a divinely composed song, one which is innately strung within the cords of tiny nerves and vessels and produces a lovely melody.

> God's divine
> ordering of our
> world continues
> in the midst of
> anything we may
> be experiencing at
> any given time.

This may seem like a lot of mumbo-jumbo, but I'll tell you why I'm writing about it. The songbird makes me think of those things that reflect cosmos in the midst of chaos, those things that reflect the harmonious order of God's creation and the Trinity. The earth and its created order reflect order in the midst of disorder. So is God's love and so is God's light. Everything God has ordained cannot be anything that it wasn't meant to be: God cannot be anything other than God. The songbird cannot not sing if it tried, much the same as we cannot survive if we don't involuntarily exchange oxygen for carbon dioxide.

Here's how I've lived this. If I had always been able to do things for my husband, Dieter, and thereby seemingly *earned* his love, I never would have known the grace of his love, his love that was there when I could do nothing, not even be there other than in bodily form. When he wrapped his arms around me, told me to go lie down, and did the dishes even though he was tired, I loved him like never before. When he answered the phone and once again declined a social invitation because he knew I wasn't up to it, even though he would have enjoyed it a great deal, I loved him like never before. I often wept, because this was a different way of being loved—it had nothing to do with what I had done for him.

The brilliance and significance of Dieter loving me as he does is that it's a human reflection of God's love for us. It isn't based on what we do for God, but on what God has already done for us, for we have already been loved through Jesus. We can count on it more than any human relationship. No matter how utterly stunning our experiences of the cosmos may be, the Trinity is always much more glorious.

Thank God that the Spirit sometimes jumps in, swarms, and envelopes us with grace. For instance, Dieter and I can often be jerky in our responses to my illness. But sometimes we get it right: I stop expecting him to read my thoughts and know what I want, and he stops wanting things to be something other than what they are. Therein we experience an exquisite calm.

The songbird does indeed sing its divinely designed song, a song that proclaims God's sovereignty and ever-present Light that will evermore infuse our darkness. For a moment or two, I know it's all right, and I love my husband like never before. Although my depression hasn't disappeared, there is cosmos in the midst of our chaos. Grace upon grace upon grace.

Ye who long pain and sorrow bear,
Praise God and on Him cast your care!
O praise Him, O praise Him!
Alleluia! Alleluia! Alleluia!
Let all things their Creator bless
And worship God in humbleness,
O praise Him! Alleluia!
Praise, praise the Father, praise the Son,
And praise the Spirit, Three in One...[53]

The world around us makes manifest the divinely ordered state of things, and we are the most glorious of all God's creations. We are the most blessedly beloved.

---

[53] St. Francis of Assisi, "All Creatures of Our God and King," 1225.

Day Forty-Five:
Redefining Good Works

Joy

You are the light of the world... let your light shine before others, so that they may see your good works and give glory to your Father in heaven. (Matthew 5:14, 16)

THERE'S LIGHT IN ME AND GOOD WORKS? WHAT?!

During these times of inner turmoil, the "good works" mentioned in Matthew 5 need to be redefined. When your mind is ill, your strength is markedly diminished and your soul is traumatized, so surely the God of great love doesn't expect you to achieve your normal level of mighty good works, to shine your usual level of brilliant wattage.

It's time to give yourself a mighty big break; it's not time to be saving the world, no matter if that world consists only of your family of four, or even one roommate. This is *your* time: delegate, relegate, and temporarily get off the committee. I promise you, people will step up to bat in your absence.

The good news, and there is always good news, is that we can still do good works that give glory to God. It's just that they look different when we're depressed. Good works during a clinical depression look like:

- getting out of bed and making it.
- brushing your teeth and hair.
- eating a balanced diet, even when you're not hungry.
- getting dressed.
- going for regular walks.
- bathing daily.
- tidying the house.
- resting.
- reading appropriate books and magazines that aren't taxing or depleting.
- asking for help.
- encouraging your partner to have a social life even if you aren't up to it.
- attending a support group or individual therapy.
- going to doctors' appointments.
- listening to someone who needs a listening ear.

- writing a card to a lonely, sad, or sick person you know.
- giving thanks for one thing, no matter how small.

It's an act of love when you do these things, because in reality they may be the absolutely last things you want to do. It is scary for your family members and friends to see you ill and hurting. Therefore, it's comforting for them to see you taking care of yourself, even in basic ways such as personal hygiene.

You are the salt of the earth and light of the world, even when you don't feel like it one bit. You retain your flavor and light despite how you feel inside. Why? Because you eternally remain a beloved child of God, no matter what. Nothing can separate you from the love of your heavenly Father—no mangled-up or depleted neurotransmitters, no low levels of serotonin, no misfiring synapses, no fun-but-exhausting mania, and definitely no diminished libido.

Matthew's gospel is full of stories about Jesus healing broken people, and that includes people with mental illnesses. Healing is here, healing is coming, and ultimate healing will happen. All is well, my brothers and sisters, all is ultimately well.

As Jesus said in the last words of Matthew, *"And remember, I am with you always, to the end of the age"* (Matthew 28:20).

So you have made it almost six weeks—way to go! Six weeks is a long time when you've been dealing with what you've had to deal with.

Why don't you take a break today? How can you celebrate? Today is a day for celebration. What does that look like for you? Does it involve people or taking a trip by yourself? Driving or walking? Cycling or taking the bus? Shopping, window shopping, or visiting thrift stores? Maybe you go to the gym for some fast, brisk exercise? How about the library or buying a brand-new book? Grocery shopping and then cooking a light meal? Baking?

Don't overdo it! Whatever it is that will bring lightness and ease, you have full permission to fill your day with it. I promise you, God delights in your delight: you are the salt of the earth and light in the world! Amen.

Day Forty-Six: God Speaks through Masters of Greek and Migraines

Joy

THE OTHER DAY I WAS READING A PAPER THAT MY SON JESSE RE-cently presented at a New Testament scholar's conference. It was titled "Expectations of Eschatological Violence in Sec-ond-Temple Judaism: The Dead Sea Scrolls, Josephus, and Implications for Jesus' Kingdom."

Just some light reading, right?

But the exciting thing was, I kind of got it! By the end of page eight, I was skittish with excitement as the penny dropped and I actually had an idea of what Jesse was saying. And it was fantastic! The scope of what a few verses in Luke were implying left me awestruck (Luke 19:41–42). In one verse, the historicity of the Jewish nation (Israel) and its past and implied future, all that which caused Jesus to weep, came together in one fell swoop. And it blew me away, rocked my socks off!

One tiny little verse in the whole Bible held all of this. Imagine! How was a mere layperson like myself supposed to pick up this holy book and trust what it was saying to me without dozens of commentaries and my scholarly son at my right hand to interpret it for me?

Well, let's leave the scholars and world of advanced exegesis for a moment and change scenes to my bedroom on a late fall afternoon. I'm curled up in a tense fetal position on my bed, the blinds are closed to the bright sunshine outside, a lavender pillow lies across my eyes, and my ears are plugged with soft foam. These are my desperate attempts to prevent incoming stimuli from penetrating my blazingly painful scalp and frazzled nervous system. I'm barely breathing: less oxygen seems to keep me less aware of my present migraine. I desperately seek solitude from people, places, and things, decisions and discussions. I want to be alone. I want to be gone.

Ah, there, I think I've reached it; I'm in the nether zone, the somewhere-out-there where the reality of life on earth isn't so razor sharp, so flippin' hard.

Hmmm, all right, I might be able to manage things if I can just stay in this zone for a while.

But it's into this exact checked-out zone that the Spirit's Word breaks through: "Alphabet."

What?

"Alphabet. Organize all your thoughts into and through the alphabet."

Hmmm. Alphabet?

Ohhh. I take in a sharp breath as I suddenly understand. It makes me smile, because this is an incarnational gift of the highest order. I'll tell you why.

At the time of this story, I haven't written for months and months because I've been unable to identify any means of organizing my thoughts. Every time I try to write, it feels like nothing more than an exercise in frustration. I don't know where to start and I don't know where to stop. Everything is mumbo-jumbo, a mess as big as the one inside my head. And *that* makes me feel crazy, and I've had enough of feeling crazy. I've left writing alone because it just makes me feel too mangled-up.

So, here it is then: the alphabet, a tangible means for creating order and tidiness. I'll organize all my thoughts and notes on depression into alphabetical categories. Oh, how I love order and tidiness. Oh, happy day! And all of this is happening right when I'm having a nine and a half out of ten migraine? *Now that just doesn't make sense!*

Jesse's paper and my alphabet migraine are all about divine revelation. Both are equally holy and of great importance. We have a merciful and loving Creator who desires to be known by us, desires to break into our stories and come alongside us. And God does this in exegetical seminars full of brilliant scholarly minds as well as in quiet, dark bedrooms occupied by frazzled minds that are feeling crazy and out of whack.

> Not one of us is
> exempt from the
> incarnational love
> of God.

Not one of us is guaranteed a lifetime exempt from depression.

Not one of us is exempt from the incarnational love of God.

Divine revelation can happen at any time to any one of us. One role of the Holy Spirit is to open our eyes to God's presence in the world around us, and to God's working in our lives in clear and distinct ways. Hallelujah! God is revealed to and known by His followers in intimate and personal ways!

May each day be filled with moments of spontaneous and glorious revelation that catch and hold you with joy! May these

Godglimpses tell you of how gloriously ordered and designed our world is, and may you rest in knowing that God is sovereign. As God is revealed and grace is known, may you be securely grounded with the blessed assurance that Jesus is yours!

Day Forty-Seven:
Touching Christ's Robe on the Edge

Suffering / Grace

SOMETIMES IT SEEMS AS IF GOD IS PLAYING A GAME OF CAT AND mouse with me. I'm the hemorrhaging woman of twelve years who is close, so very, very close, to touching the hem of Christ's robe, only to have Him snatch it away at the absolute last millisecond like the lion tamer's crackling whip. Mile after dusty mile I crawl feebly, ever failingly, stretching my screaming and exhausted limbs, wanting only to touch His robe and know joy.

Of course, this isn't what happened in the real Bible story. This is what's happening in the thoughts of my depressed mind. In the biblical narrative, the nameless woman does indeed reach her goal and graze Christ's tunic. Immediately, she feels the flow stop.[54] Rather than sharply rebuking her, which would have been culturally expected, Jesus calls her a daughter and proclaims that it is her faith that has made her well. Some in the crowd would have called her obstinate and rebellious, because according to Jewish law she had just defiled Jesus. But no, Jesus focused only on her faith, her essence.

Calling her his daughter, Jesus implies connection and protection. Imagine what this meant to someone who had been shut away and shunned from society for twelve long and lonely years. The fact that this woman even presented herself in the crowd was blasphemous. Realistically, she should have expected punishment rather than Christ's beautiful pardon.

It can be said that faith is a life-and-death matter at times. Author Virginia Stem Owens claims, "When we approach God, however hesitantly, we are always teetering on the margin of life whether we recognize it or not. Faith never comes alive except on the edge."[55]

There's no doubt about it: depression takes us to the edge. And I guess Owens would say that therein lies a gift of depression—on the edge, we meet Jesus and He calls us son

---

[54] Having bled constantly for seven months myself, not twelve years, I can wholeheartedly believe how gloriously redeeming this must have felt for this woman.

[55] Virginia Stem Owens, *Daughters of Eve: Women of the Bible Speak to Women of Today* (Colorado Springs, CO: NavPress Publishing Group, 1995), 92–93.

or daughter. He tells us that our faith has made us well. How full of blessing!

> The lap of luxury stifles faith; emotional self-sufficiency smothers it. That's why it's always the marginal people Jesus notices. Not only this woman but the widow who put her two pennies - all she had - into the temple treasury. If the woman with the issue of blood had not already spent all her money on doctors, she might still have clung to the hope that they could cure her. The end of our rope is where we're always closest to God.[56]

Do you feel at the end of your rope today? Blessings of courage to you, for this is where you can meet God. What is it that you need Jesus' healing for today? Are you stretching to touch the hem of His robe? Be not afraid, for He will stop, turn, and meet your eyes. And in those eyes you will see His love, and in your ears you will hear Him call you daughter, call you son, and you will sense the flow of pain subside as you no longer feel quite so alone.

---

[56] Ibid.

Blessings on you, child of Yahweh. You are eternally loved. Go in the knowledge that you do not walk on by yourself, that the love of the Father, the friendship of the Son, and the comfort of the Holy Spirit go with you, now and forever. Amen.

Day Forty-Eight: May God's Peace Reign Grandly in Your Brain

Comfort

THIS IS MY BENEDICTION FOR YOU TODAY. I PRAY IT WILL COMFORT and bless.

May our gracious and eternal Lord gather you into God's arms and hold you as the dear and beloved child that you are. In your mind's fog, may your eyes be powerfully focused upon Yahweh. May God's peace reign grandly within your brain, dispelling all your confusion and pain. May the Almighty be your vision, may your weary soul be rested, and may God breathe gentle mercy upon you. May Jesus' loving kindness break into your unknowing so that you will know deeply of God's care for you. May each and every breath be calmed and evened out, so that, stilled in the Spirit, any and all agitation may cease. May Jesus take your hand into His own and be your Shepherd, as He longs to do.

May the Spirit of comfort lead you into God's presence to live a whole and joyous moment with the Three in One, a moment to which you may return time and again during what may be difficult days ahead. Know that through it all you will be held and kept in the promises of God. You are precious in the Lord's sight; you are honored and you are loved. Do not be afraid, for you have been redeemed; your Creator calls you by name. You belong. On the Almighty rests your deliverance and honor. Your mighty rock, your refuge, is in God. Yes, you will go out with joy![57]

---

[57] A paraphrase of Isaiah 43:4, 41:1, Psalm 62:10, and Isaiah 55:12.

Day Forty-Nine: God's Truth Rings in the Tempest's Roar

Grace

BEFORE READING TODAY'S REFLECTION, I ENCOURAGE YOU TO RE-
view the lyrics to "My Life Flows On" from Day Forty.[58] Life
does flow on, even in the midst of deep, strife-filled tumult.
It amazes me that there is a song to be found even when my
cries of joy are snuffed out and my hearing is a dull, hollow
echo. Is this the songbird's song? Is it the blessed rightness
to God's kingdom here on earth that remains even when all
seems wrong in mine?

Somehow, somewhere, the song keeps playing beneath
the raging turmoil. Way beneath the anguish and lamentation,

<hr>

[58] Or better still, listen to a recording of Enya singing it.

there is a real hymn. Though it may be far off, it hails a new creation. New creation speaks to me of new beginnings of hope in the midst of pain, of surges of energy in the midst of fatigue and desoluteness, and purpose and worth in the soul-sureness of uselessness.

Can you hear it echo in your very own soul?

Can you hear God's truth ringing in the tempest's roar?

Cling to the Rock, for the storms cannot ultimately shake our inmost calm, and ultimately we cannot keep from singing, because love is the Lord of heaven and earth and joy is the ultimate victor.

We are an Easter people and this is resurrection hope. Cling to the Light that the darkness cannot snuff out. Your very being contains this Light, even when everything feels so very dark. Hope is rising with the Spirit's roar of proclamation: I am, and I will never leave you. Amen, amen, and amen.

Week Eight

Day Fifty:
Master, Wake Up, We Are Perishing!

Suffering

The soul has to go on loving in the emptiness, or at least go on wanting to love, though it may only be with an infinitesimal part of itself. Then, one day, God will come to show himself to this soul and reveal the beauty of the world to it. It is often in periods of seeming fruitlessness that Jesus Christ reveals his power, and in times of darkness that God sheds the greatest light.[59]

—Simone Weil

[59] Simone Weil, "Waiting for God," *Spiritual Formation Bible: Growing in Intimacy with God through Scripture* (Grand Rapids, MI: Zondervan, 1999), 1357.

IN MATTHEW 8, WE READ OF THE DISCIPLES TAKING OFF WITH Jesus in a boat as they withdrew from a large crowd wherein they had witnessed their Teacher perform many healing miracles. They were all exhausted, but also somewhat wired, it seems, because Jesus was the only one who immediately fell asleep—and He fell *deeply* asleep, for even the great raging storm that soon erupted failed to waken Him.

The disciples became frightfully nervous and anxious, but Jesus slept on. No longer able to contain themselves, they woke him, shouting, "Master, we are perishing! Save us now!"

In the midst of a depressive episode, especially one accompanied by severe migraines, I, too, shout at the Lord, "Master, I am perishing! Master, do you not care? Do you sleep on, untroubled at your child's distress, untroubled that my heart is so wrenched? Do you sleep on, not caring that anxiety riddles my nighttime hours so that sleep never rests my exhausted soul?"

I feel overtaken, almost suffocated by the pain of downward heaviness. I plead with my Maker to deliver me from this intolerable affliction. I ask God, "Where are you? Are you sleeping?" I beg my Lord to wake up because *I cannot stand it anymore*. I feel so bereft of soul during such weeks. Thoughts of shame churn and churn, shouting accusingly of how I don't measure up. I'm tossed to and fro in raging waters of dread that pummel my psyche.

"You are no good," I hear. "You are worth nothing at all because you can do nothing at all."

Messages of soul-sucking shame thunder in my ears and ruin my days. I storm around the house like a walking, talking thundercloud. And I yell and yell and yell—silently, explosively, inside my head, at myself, and at my God that I may be saved.

All the while, my heart is battered. Bruised. And all this while it becomes smaller. Sometimes it barely contracts; at other times it beats like furious waves crashing against the boulders that line the shore.

These are the things I'm most poignantly aware of, things that are in the forefront of my mind and experience.

But oddly, I catch glimpses in the corners of my consciousness of something else that's undeniably, albeit mysteriously, happening at the same time. Christ has awakened and ordered the storm calmed. My heart becomes still and, strangely, it seems it has also become cultivated and tilled during the storm, as if the storm itself has prepared the soil of my constricted heart and deposited kingdom seeds of resurrection. These seeds have taken root immediately and deeply and speak of all things being made new, of tears drying up, of joy coming with the morning even though the night has been very long (Psalm 30:5). These kingdom seeds speak of never being forsaken or left alone, and they speak of stories being redeemed.

As Father John O'Donahue once wrote,

When the reverberations of shock subside in you, may grace come to restore you to balance. May it shape a new space in your heart. To embrace this illness as a teacher who has come to open your life to new worlds.[60]

Seven weeks have passed now. Will you celebrate? Will it be a hard, hard day because you aren't feeling all that much better? In this past time of darkness, have you seen some windows of light? Have you seen some notes of God's grace? What has kept you through these seven weeks? What, or who, has stilled your storms? What state would you say your heart is in—softened or hardened?

If you're only feeling slightly better, or not feeling better at all, clinically, I sit with you in that. I know how it feels, as I've been there several times. I found it dark, extremely disappointing, and exhausting. How do you start all over again? I discovered that I needed to rely on a few key people, especially my doctor, to remind me

---

60 O'Donahue, *To Bless the Space Between Us*, 60.

of things like delegating tasks, taking one day at a time, decreasing responsibilities, and taking a walk each day.[61]

This is a time to regroup and take good, good care of yourself. Buoy yourself up. While continuing to hold your deep disappointment, can you identify moments of God's grace? Light a Christ-candle in celebration of that.

If you're feeling a whole lot better, Hallelujah! Thank God. Thank those who have supported you. Thank God for researchers and medications. Thank yourself for taking good care of you. Celebrate!

---

[61] For a more complete list, review Day Ten.

Day Fifty-One:
God's Intention Is Life

Suffering

WHERE IS GOD IN OUR SUFFERING? HOW DO WE FIND GOD IN OUR suffering? *Is* God in our suffering?

When I need to find answers to the big questions of suffering, I go to the story of Christ's big suffering: the week of Passion which led to His crucifixion. This was a week of betrayals, rejections, mockery, lashings, and—most devastating of all—the silence of God.

I find it difficult to stay with Christ from Palm Sunday through Good Friday. It is a time of agony and tortuous suffering, loneliness and betrayal by best friends. Ironically, however, it is through this kind of time that we see the true essence of our God.

As pastor and author Nadia Bolz-Weber has boldly proclaimed,

> This is our God... Not a distant judge nor a sadist, but a God who weeps. A God who suffers, not only for us, but with us. Nowhere is the presence of God amidst suffering more salient than on the cross. Therefore, what can I do but confess that this is not a God who causes suffering? This is a God who bears suffering.
>
> I need to believe that God does not initiate suffering; God transforms it. [62]

God is a God of transformation and redemption. God takes our pain and makes beauty and wholeness out of it. Maybe not right away, but someday.

> God takes our pain
> and makes beauty
> and wholeness out
> of it.

---

[62] Nadia Bolz-Weber, *Pastrix: The Cranky, Beautiful Faith of a Sinner and Saint* (New York: NY, Jericho Books), 128.

The Bible doesn't spell everything out, word for word, so we do well to ask, "What is God's intention?" Throughout the Bible, from the Old Testament to the New, God's intention is life: resurrected life, abundant life. We can count on this, you and I. Even in boats caught in a raging storm, Jesus is with us. Even if asleep, He remains: Emmanuel. Even if asleep, He transforms all heaven and earth.

Bolz-Weber wrote,

> I realized that in Jesus, God had come to dwell with us and share our human story. Even the parts of our human story that are the most painful. God was not sitting in heaven looking down at Jesus' life and death and cruelly allowing his son to suffer. God was not looking down on the cross. God was hanging *from* the cross. God had entered our pain and loss and death so deeply and took all of it into God's own self so that we might know who God really is.[63]

Jesus is the crucified Christ, yes, but the week of Passion ends in a glorious, eternal resurrection!

---

[63] Ibid., 86.

As Jesus told the sea, He says to you now, "Be calm." Know that all is ultimately well. Gently tell yourself that you are in the middle of a storm and that you're having a hard time. If you don't know how to do this alone, just quietly admit this and let it be.

Place your right hand gently on top of your heart and let it rest there for a moment. Breathe freshly oxygenated blood into it. Drop your shoulders and relax. As you breathe, remember that this depression is something you're experiencing; it is not what you are. It is not your identity.

As you go forward into today, place your right hand over your heart and breathe deeply, softly, whenever you feel your pulse quicken and your breathing become shallow. Even if just for a few breaths. Every little bit helps. Bless you!

Day Fifty-Two: Blessings Sweeter Because of the Bitter Sting

Grace

ON THE NIGHT OF JESUS' ARREST WHEN THE REGIMENT CAME TO the garden to seize Him, two hundred powerful soldiers staggered backwards and fell as they met God, the Word made flesh. It is a terrifying thing to come into contact with the Holy One. *Mysterium tremendum* is a terrifying mystery in which God appears and we are terrified and attracted, drawn and repelled.

When I "get" God—can anyone ever, really?—when I'm aware that the Spirit has somehow managed to get me to let go of my ironclad grasp on my life, I most often weep. I weep because I've gained a sliver of insight into the Light of the world. In its beam, I become aware of how short I fall of God's glory. And then, just before I think I'm about to be exiled, grace swoops in and does its work. Oh, hallelujah! Hallelujah!

Ironically, I more often encounter God in this way when I'm depressed. I think it's because I'm so exhausted that my fingers start to uncurl of their own volition. Besides, I have no more fight in me. I have no words, so I don't try to rationalize or intellectualize what I'm experiencing. Rather, there's the vacuous, beige void of numbness, the thoughts of "Oh, what's the use of doing anything?"

And so I surrender. I'm in a place where I almost have no choice but to surrender.

But you see, herein lies the blessing of the curse. When I'm not depressed, I have a firm hold on my life.[64] I'm such a type-A personality that I plan, place, and perfect everything I do. Only when I'm weak do I begin to allow God to really permeate my thick skin and take up residence. This is a fact, and I'm sorry for it. It happens time and time again; it's unfortunate and makes me sad. Lamentably, it seems that only when suffering do I become vulnerable enough to reach certain depths of communion with God, and therefore levels of healing.

On the surface, it astounds me that I don't pray for complete healing. On second thought, though, I believe

---

[64] Well, I'm seduced by the thought that I have a firm hold.

it makes sense: while the *mysterium tremendum* can be terrifying, it is full of blessing at the same time.

I invite you to think of your depression in much the same way. Try as hard as you can to receive it, as terrifying as it can be, and to think of it as holding blessings—blessings sweeter because of the bitter, biting sting.

Cry out! Cry out! As one living in the wilderness, cry out to your God who will not leave you as chaff. Just cry out, even if silently, no matter what it is you want to scream or whimper. God can handle it. God can manage God.

May you be filled today with good courage so that you may breathe deeply of the indwelling Spirit, the Spirit that will keep you in the midst of your terror and move you from a place of fear into one of love, move you to the next minute, the next hour, and through the long night.

Day Fifty-Three:
Convicted by Doom

Comfort

I WAS TWENTY-FOUR YEARS OLD WHEN I GAVE BIRTH TO OUR SON, and twenty-six when our daughter was born. This meant that our children weren't introduced to computers, iPhones, and other screens at a very early age. PlayStation was the big thing when they were entering adolescence, and it was a big thrill when we allowed them to rent it for the weekend. It wasn't a common occurrence in our household.

So when our son's friend offered to loan him his own PlayStation, Jesse was overjoyed. "Can I borrow it, Mom? Dad? Can I have it for the weekend? *Please?*"

We decided it would be okay for a weekend, provided his usage was limited to a certain amount of time and only after chores and homework were done. Jesse was in heaven!

On the market at the time was a widely popular game called *Doom*. At the time, I didn't know much about the intricate details or goals of the game, but I soon became aware of a personality change that came over Jesse and the darkness that descended upon our family room. After only a day of its lodging, I decided the game had to go. It had grown much bigger than a mere plastic cassette; it was a lingering and menacing presence that made me angry as a pacifist and protective as a mom. Violence was the operative theme, and killing, guns, and slaughtering were the goals.

Coming to the decision that the game had to go wasn't easy for me. I'm one who avoids conflict, especially at this time in my life, so I ruminated over the *Doom* issue. Was it really that bad? Was it going to wreck Jesse to play for a weekend?

Just let it go, I thought. *Don't be so uptight. You're imagining things. Everything's all right, the family room's the family room, same as always, just like Jess is the same guy as always.*

On and on my thoughts ran, emptying me of the confidence and ability to make a decision.

Somehow, probably because of all the prayers I prayed, my wits came about me. When Jess came home from school that day, I asked him to join me upstairs in the den. I told him that I had been feeling creeped out when I walked through the family room, how it had seemed really dark to me and oppressive. I remarked how he and I had seemed to be kind of impatient with each other, too, and I asked if he'd noticed these things as well. He said that he had. I told him that I thought it had a lot to do with the violent game.

He became very still.

I asked him his thoughts about the game and if he enjoyed playing it.

"Kind of," he said. "Not really."

"Jess, the game has to go. Today."

"Okay, Mom."

"Jess?"

"Mmhmm?"

"Do you consider yourself a Christian?"

"Yeah."

"Then I think, as Christians, we have some decisions to make. And I think that, with each decision, we either add to the light of the world or take away from it."

His eyes got pretty big. "You really believe that, Mom? Really?"

"Yes, Jess, I really believe that."

May the tangling of rumination unfurl today, so that you gain some sense of clarity.

And may you be greatly blessed with wisdom and courage in the decisions you want to make. May you listen to and receive your feelings as the good and holy teachers they are, going forth honoring that which you have learned from grieving the losses you now know.

May strength and humor guide you and a grounded backbone lead the way in doing what you know to be right and true and good. Blessings on you, and may God keep you well. And so it is. Amen.

Day Fifty-Four: Is Life a Wonderful Balance of Both/And?

Grace

Joy and sorrow are never separated. When our hearts rejoice at a spectacular view, we may miss our friends who cannot see it, and when we are overwhelmed with grief, we may discover what true friendship is all about. Joy is hidden in sorrow and sorrow in joy. If we try to avoid sorrow at all costs, we may never taste joy, and if we are suspicious of ecstasy, agony can never reach us either. Joy and sorrow are the parents of our spiritual growth.

—Henri Nouwen[65]

[65] Henri Nouwen, *Bread for the Journey: A Daybook of Wisdom and Faith*

DAYS AND WEEKS HAVE NOW PASSED AND WE ARE NEARING THE end of our eight-week time together. Throughout this writing, it has struck me again how full of both gifts and losses an episode of depression can be. A month after it has finished, I usually find myself crying all over again as I grieve the losses that each single episode of depression has brought: the loss of family time, loss of work and creativity, loss of social connection with loved ones, loss of purpose and direction, loss of memory and focus, loss of self and a sense of mastery, loss of energy and predictability, loss of power, and lots, lots more. Predominantly, a loss of hope. And mixed in with all of it, a good dollop of fear. Fear of never coming back and a fear of insanity.

Not much in our western culture encourages us to embrace such darkness. No. As Barbara Brown Taylor wrote,

> ...eliminating darkness is pretty high on the human agenda—not just physical darkness but also metaphysical darkness, which includes psychological, emotional, relational, and spiritual darkness... Fear is the main thing. Almost everyone is afraid of being afraid.[66]

As you know by having read this book, I have felt fear. But I have also found there to be many gifts inherent in

(San Francisco, CA: HarperCollins, 1997), January 2.
[66] Barbara Brown Taylor, *Learning to Walk in the Dark* (New York, NY: HarperCollins, 2014), 4.

the darkness of depression. These gifts have changed the meaning of my life and my hope for the future. Taylor added,

> I have learned things in the dark that I could never have learned in the light, things that have saved my life over and over again, so that there is really only one logical conclusion. I need darkness as much as I need light.[67]

Meister Eckhart, a fourteenth-century mystic, once wrote, "The soul does not grow by addition but by subtraction."[68] The Lord knows how much of life is subtracted during an episode of depression. But we do well to take time to ponder the soul growth that occurs at the same time—the moments where we perhaps hear the Spirit groaning inwardly, graciously presenting before God that for which we have no words. Think of the times of utter powerlessness you have felt. Could they become moments on the "other side," the side of quiet and stillness and God-perfection? Of ease and all-rightness and trust?

Our culture is so very dualistic. It's either this or that, black or white, night or day. But what if it's both/and? What if it's black *and* white, this *and* that, night *and* day? That would be a lovely balance. Even though we cannot see as well at night as during the day, it is, after all, the time for slowing down and resting.

[67] Ibid., 5.
[68] Ibid., 179.

"Yes, but," I used to vehemently complain, "slowing down is the last thing I want to do. Slowing down makes all the things I've stuffed down out of mind come to the surface and I have to think about them."

Well, whether I like it or not, depression has made me slow down and offered me ample time to rest. This resting is hard, hard work. But healing has come, and my soul has grown. Grown in the night. I now, and only now, really know that I am loved. Just because I am.

Nowadays, I don't embrace depression in open, loving arms, but I don't hate it and myself when it comes my way. I try to honor its space in my life. I try. With everything in me, I try.

Oh, who am I fooling?

I *really* don't like it at all, and I doubt I ever will. Maybe it's better to say that I don't shame myself so terribly and become depressed over my depression. I believe I can do this mostly because I can now accept the truth that life holds much loss, and I am no longer so very angry about that.[69]

Here you are, dear friend, nearing the very end of eight weeks. Celebrate colorfully for how well you have made it to this day!

[69] I can now say that I'm no longer so angry about much of my life being about loss. This is a result of many things and many years spent in counselling therapy. I've received excellent care—medically, psychologically, physically, and spiritually—and the undying love of family and friends over a long period of time. My heart overflows with gratitude.

Light the candle on your beautiful plate to honor this journey.[70] Reflect upon your understanding of your depression and sit with compassion for your story.[71] Let the Spirit flow over what is very uniquely yours, in and out and over, flowing grace and mercy. Blessings to you, now and always, now and always. Amen.

---

[70] See Day Twenty-One.
[71] See Day Five.

Day Fifty-Five:
The Triumph Song of Life

Joy

HERE YOU ARE WITH ONLY TWO DAYS TO GO IN YOUR EIGHT-WEEK journey, and you are at your own unique place. I pray that you are in a more secure and rested place than when you started. I do hope that you are stronger and healthier in all ways. I hope grace is a constant companion, and I wish you a strong heart and good courage. May faith undergird your steps as you go forward from here. May you be kissed by hope every faltering moment of each day, and may those benedicted moments turn into hours, and those hours into days eternal.

Love *is* the Lord of heaven and earth. I hope this makes you sing! The same gentle and immeasurable power that empowered Christ to turn toward Jerusalem, knowing that Jerusalem meant His death, is the power that will hold and keep you. You are loved, my friend, you are so greatly loved.

May you be revived again and again, your heart filled with love. May the breath of the Holy Spirit bid the fears and sorrows of your soul to depart, and may you be sheltered under the protective holy wings of Yahweh as you are sustained. Surely God's goodness and mercy shall attend you every day. You borrow life from God and, as such, you are ever in the Eternal's care. There is no place in life or level of darkness that God will not go to find you. Hallelujah, Emmanuel!

So, my friend, as we end today I invite you to join the mighty chorus:

Mortals, join the mighty chorus,
Which the morning stars began;
God's own love is reigning o'er us,
Joining people hand in hand.
Ever singing, march we onward,
Victors in the midst of strife;
Joyful music lifts us sunward
In the triumph song of life.[72]

---

[72] Henry Van Dyke, "Joyful, Joyful, We Adore Thee," 1907.

Day Fifty-Six:
A Closing Prayer of Benediction for Us All

Grace/Comfort

Lift up our souls above the weary round of harassing thoughts to thy eternal presence. Lift up our minds to the pure, bright serene atmosphere of thy presence, that we may breathe freely, there repose in thy love, there be at rest from ourselves and from all things that weary us: and thence return, arrayed in thy peace, to do and to bear whatsoever shall best please thee, O blessed Lord.[73]

—E.B. Pusey

[73] E.B. Pusey, *The Oxford Book of Prayer* (New York, NY: Oxford University Press, 1985), 80.

The peace of the Father of joy,
The peace of the Christ of life,
The peace of the Spirit of grace,
To ourselves and to our children,
Ourselves and our children.[74]

---

[74] Carmina Gadelica, "The peace of the Father..." *The Printery House*. Date of access: March 19, 2018 (https://www.printeryhouse.org/ProdPage. asp?prod=CA5007).

Appendix One: Emergency Contacts

IF YOU ARE SUICIDAL OR WANTING TO HURT YOURSELF:

- Call the crisis line or go to the emergency room of your local hospital. *Tell them you are having suicidal thoughts or are wanting to hurt yourself.* This important information will help ensure that you get the attention you need and deserve.
- Tell someone who is able to get you the help you need how you are feeling.
- Contact the SAFER Suicide Attempt Counselling Service: (604) 675-3985. This isn't just for suicide attempts; it's also for those having thoughts of suicide.
- Call the Kids helpline: (800) 668-6868 (in Canada).

- Visit www.save.org, a website for suicide prevention, information, and awareness.
- Call SAVE (Suicide Awareness Voices of Education) at 1-800-273-TALK (or text 8255).

For Vancouver residents only:

- Access and Assessment. This is a twenty-four-hour, seven days per week care facility for those with mental health and substance abuse needs. It's located at 711 West Twelfth Avenue. Call 604-875-8289 (also a support telephone line).
- Mood Disorders Association, a holistic group of healthcare professionals. Call (604) 873-0103 or visit at 1450-605 Robson Street.

Appendix Two: Assertive Statements

1. When someone wants you to do something but you're too exhausted, you could say something like, "I'm really not up to going out/having people over/having sex, etc. I know you'd really like to, and this is disappointing for you. Can we try for tomorrow?"

2. If your partner/spouse/roommate wants to do something with you, for example have a dinner party, and asks you about it in the morning, you could say, "I'm feeling pretty tired already, but I'd really like to do this. It seems important to you. How can we manage our time by doing things together to make it happen? What needs to be done? What can you do and what can I do?"

3. If you're feeling agitated and irritable and need some space, say, "I'm feeling really agitated and irritable right now because of my illness (because of the side effects of my medication/because I'm not feeling well). I'd really appreciate you cutting me some slack for a bit. Thank you."

4. If you have kids older than toddlers and need some time alone, say, "Mommy/Daddy needs some quiet time so s/he's going to lie on the couch and close her/his eyes. Everything's okay, you don't need to worry. If you have a very, very important thing you need to ask me or tell me, you can, but only if it can't wait until I'm finished. I'm going to set the timer for fifteen minutes. When the buzzer goes, we can do something together. Is there anything you need to tell me or ask me now before I set the timer? Okay, I know you can do this, and it's going to help Mommy/Daddy so much."

5. Remember that saying no is always an option, and you don't owe everyone a lengthy account as to why you've said it. Politely and simply state that at this time it's not going to work out. If you like, you can say that you're sorry this is so, and you know that it's disappointing to them. If the activity is something you would really have liked to do, ask the person to please ask you again in the (near) future.

Daily Readings by Theme

Comfort

Taking Heart	3
Like Any Other Organ, Your Brain May Sometimes Need Help	6
Is God Allowing My Suffering?	20
A Psychiatric Disease, Not a Personality Flaw	22
The World's Standards or God's?	157
May God's Peace Reign Grandly in Your Brain	186
Convicted by Doom	204
A Closing Prayer of Benediction for Us All	215

Grace

All Tatted-Up with Grace	38
Whisper to Me of Who I Truly Am	44
Acting on Your Principles Rather than on Your Feelings	51

Our Highest and Truest Calling	63
Honoring Three-Week Cracks of Light	69
Well-Loved and Chosen	78
On Your Knees	81
What Will You Choose to Choose?	87
Holy and Beautiful	91
Uncurled, Surrendering Fists	95
Touching Base with the Basics Again	103
At the End of Your Rope and Being Not Afraid	112
Anger-Filled Disillusions and the Mystery that Is Life with God	116
Even in the Silence of God	128
God Has Not Come to a Full Stop	133
The Fear that Is Your Cross Is Also the Cross that Leads to Life	140
Songs in the Night He Giveth	149
Spirit Whisperings of Healthful Change	164
Cosmos in the Midst of Chaos	169
God's Truth Rings in the Tempest's Roar	188
Blessings Sweeter Because of the Bitter Sting	201
Is Life a Wonderful Balance of Both/And?	208
A Closing Prayer of Benediction for Us All	215

Hope

Uncurled, Surrendering Fists	95
Five Weeks and Hanging in There	122
Spear- and Nail-Pierced Wounds Embrace Our Bruised Hearts	145
Lifted Up Above All that Terrifies You	155

Information

Like Any Other Organ, Your Brain May Sometimes Need Help	6
A Chapter of Medication-Taking	9
Medications and Psychological Therapy	12
So How Did This All Start?	16
A Psychiatric Disease, Not a Personality Flaw	22
A Small, Manageable Task	26
The Wonders of Walking	28
A Game Plan	30
Thoughts of Dying	34
The State of Your States	41
Acting on Your Principles Rather than on Your Feelings	51
The Tried and True Twosome—Medication and Therapy	55
Ceaseless Choices and Dizzying Decision-Making	58
Where Did That Thought Come From?	72
May Your Deep Questions Lead to Places of Peace	84
What Will You Choose to Choose?	87
Living the Best Possible Way with Our Emotions	100
Touching Base with the Basics Again	103
What Makes You Uniquely You?	108
Five Weeks and Hanging in There	122
Even in the Silence of God	128
Touching Christ's Robe on the Edge	182

Joy

Sassy Powerlessness!   106

The Fear that Is Your Cross Is Also the Cross that Leads to Life   140

Songs in the Night He Giveth   149

Cosmos in the Midst of Chaos   169

Redefining Good Works   173

God Speaks through Masters of Greek and Migraines   177

The Triumph Song of Life   213

Suffering

Is God Allowing My Suffering?   20

Thoughts of Dying   34

All the Courage You Have Ever Had to Muster   48

Dying Does Not Make Perfect Sense   66

On Your Knees   81

Anger-Filled Disillusions and the Mystery that Is Life with God   116

Spear- and Nail-Pierced Wounds Embrace Our Bruised Hearts   145

Lifted Up Above All that Terrifies You   155

Touching Christ's Robe on the Edge   182

Master, Wake Up, We Are Perishing!   192

God's Intention Is Life   197

Shorter Readings

Like Any Other Organ, Your Brain May Sometimes Need Help   6

A Chapter of Medication-Taking   9

Is God Allowing My Suffering?   20

A Psychiatric Disease, Not a Personality Flaw   22

A Small, Manageable Task   26

The Wonders of Walking   28

Whisper to Me of Who I Truly Am   44

Dying Does Not Make Perfect Sense   66

Honoring Three-Week Cracks of Light   69

Well-Loved and Chosen   78

May Your Deep Questions Lead to Places of Peace   84

Living the Best Possible Way with Our Emotions   100

Touching Base with the Basics Again   103

At the End of Your Rope and Being Not Afraid   112

Lifted Up Above All that Terrifies You   155

God's Intention Is Life   197

Recommended Reading

Novels

Maria de los Santos, *Love Walked In* (New York, NY: Penguin Group, 2006).

Juliette Faye, *Shelter Me* (New York, NY: HarperCollins, 2009).

Kent Haruf, *Benediction* (New York, NY: Vintage Books, 2014).

Jo-Ann Mapson, *Hank and Chloe* (New York, NY: HarperCollins, 1994).

Louise Penny, *Still Life* (London, UK: Sphere, 2005). Note that this is the first of the Armand Gamache mystery novels, and I recommend them all.

Faith / Theology

David G. Benner, *The Gift of Being Yourself: The Sacred Call to Self-Discovery* (Downers Grove, IL: InterVarsity Press, 2004).

Sarah Bessey, *Jesus Feminist: An Invitation to Revisit the Bible's View of Women* (New York, NY: Howard Books, 2004).

Barbara Brown Taylor, *Learning to Walk in the Dark* (New York, NY: HarperCollins, 2014).

Frederick Buechner, *Sacred Journey: A Memoir of Early Days* (New York, NY: Harper, 1982).

Frederick Buechner, *Now and Then: A Memoir of Vocation* (New York, NY: Harper, 1983).

Frederick Buechner, *Telling Secrets: A Memoir* (New York, NY: Harper, 1991).

Robert Farrar Capon, *The Mystery of Christ and Why We Don't Get It* (Grand Rapids, MI: Eerdmans Publishing Group, 1993).

Ann Lamott, *Help, Thanks, Wow: The Three Essential Prayers* (New York, NY: Riverhead Books, 2012).

Ann Lamott, *Plan B: Further Thoughts on Faith* (New York, NY: Riverhead Books, 2005).

Madeline L'Engle, *And It Was Good: Reflections on Beginnings* (Wheaton, IL: Harold Saw Publishers, 1983).

Henri Nouwen, *Seeds of Hope: Thoughts to Nourish a New Spirituality* (New York, NY: Bantam Books, 1989).

Henri Nouwen, *Turn My Mourning into Dancing: Finding Hope in Hard Times* (Nashville, TN: Thomas Nelson, 2001).

Eugene Peterson, *Living the Message* (New York, NY: Harper, 1996).

Autobiography

Martha Manning, *Undercurrents: A Therapist's Reckoning with Her Own Depression* (New York, NY: HarperCollins, 1994)

Parenting

Ann E. Caron, *Don't Stop Loving Me: A Reassuring Guide for Mothers of Adolescent Daughters* (New York, NY: Harper Perennial, 1992).

Barbara Coloroso, *Kids Are Worth It!* (Toronto, ON: Somerville House Publishing, 1994).

Deborah MacNamara, *Rest, Play, Grow: Making Sense of Preschoolers (or Anyone who Acts Like One)* (Vancouver, BC: Aona Books, 2016)

Adele Faber and Elaine Mazlish, *How to Talk So Kids Will Listen and Listen So Kids Will Talk* (New York, NY: Avon Books, 1980